Contents

Introduction   1

Chapter 1
Rare Vapours, Rumbling Volcanoes and
Simmer Dim   13

Twilight Diary – Winter   38

Chapter 2
Zeitgebers, Blind Ducks and Seeing Ghosts   57

Twilight Diary – Spring   87

Chapter 3
Dusk Perfume, Dead Flesh Flowers and
Picky Sheep   117

Twilight Diary – Spring/Summer   136

Chapter 4
Cock Crow and Sparrow's Fart					155

Twilight Diary – Summer				174

Chapter 5
The Greatest Show on Earth				191

Twilight Diary – Autumn				209

Chapter 6
Dawn Births, Neanderthal DNA and
Upside-Down Moths						229

Notes									249
Acknowledgements						266
Index									267

Introduction

As a child, I slept under the stars. My bedroom was an attic at the top of a tall Victorian house, and my bed lay directly beneath a vast cast-iron skylight. Its glass was thin and wobbly, dissected down the middle by a glazing bar, and I would spend hours lying on my back, staring through it.

With no landmarks to look at directly up through the roof window, the changing sky provided all the view I needed. At night, I would fall asleep to the sky's darkening. In the early hours, I was woken by the gentle brightening of the dawn. Once a servant's room, there was never any attempt to shade the skylight in the attic or provide a homely curtain. A young nineteenth-century domestic would have been expected to wake before dawn anyway, and probably been so tired, after a day of grafting, she'd have fallen straight into the sleep of the dead, regardless of any residual light.

Even as I lay rolled up in a dense woollen blanket with my eyelids tight shut, I could sense the daylight's growing intensity. The colossally heavy skylight was often propped open with a crude metal strap. It held the window ajar just enough for a morning breeze to float in and drift slowly down onto my face and pillow. The birds woke with sunrise too. Many chimed in even earlier, when the sky seemed too dark for any bird to bother. As daylight's intensity increased, so did the chorus. Robins first, then blackbirds and thrushes – the piccolos of the orchestra – soon followed by the percussive beats of the chiffchaff and great tit.

Even as a small child I knew there was something special about twilight. Every day, in the period of time just before sunrise and straight after sunset, magic happens. Dawn is morning's twilight, dusk the evening's. Not once, but twice a day, the atmosphere is partially illuminated by a sun that's hiding below the horizon, creating a sky that magically glows with soft, diffused light.

Now, as an adult, that love affair continues. Living as I do, on a smallholding at the bottom of a North Yorkshire valley, in a farmhouse that faces directly south, I experience dawn and dusk in its many iterations. For a good portion of the year, I'm up before sunrise, traipsing the dog around the barns or feeding the various crowing and bleating flocks scattered around the farm. I'm

INTRODUCTION

even more likely to see dusk, an event that takes on a completely different character depending on the season.

And yet, how many of us truly know what goes on in those precious moments between dark and clear? Circadian rhythms - those internal clocks that keep our bodies running on time - affect almost all living things, including animals, plants, and even microbes. They, of course, profoundly affect us too. The gentle shift in the intensity and colour of light that happens only during twilight is probably the most important cue that keeps the natural world running smoothly. Earth is also one of the few planets that has twilight. As we'll learn later in this book, for twilight to exist you need sunlight scattering through a dense, dusty atmosphere. Imagine living on the Moon - cocooned in a layer of gases so wispy and tenuous that scientists can't even bring themselves to call it an atmosphere, referring to it instead as an 'exosphere'. There, the transition from day to night is instant, as if someone suddenly turned the lights out.

A unique set of animals makes the most of dawn and dusk. While those who come out at night are 'nocturnal', and day dwellers 'diurnal', twilight creatures have a niche and a word of their own - 'crepuscular'. In the blushing light, when the Sun is near rising or hidden just below the horizon, many different forms of life begin their busiest times. With just enough light to see, but not quite enough light to be seen, the twilight offers both temporal safety and a unique veil for hunting. Eyes blindfolded, other senses come into their own – scent, hearing, touch and taste.

In the countryside, hedgehogs, barn owls and bats are perhaps our best-known crepuscular creatures, but many hedgerow, pond and woodland animals live life on the day's margins – from frogs to foxes, otters to blackbirds, the half-light provides rich pickings and golden opportunities. Even our most pampered pets and domesticated farm animals – who seemingly fall in line with human routines – retain their crepuscular streak. Cats, cows and chickens are all still influenced by the power of twilight.

Sheep too. There have been plenty of twilight births on our smallholding, and our lambers' uniform is typically pyjamas hidden by a thick coat and wellies. I've lost count of the times we've had to help a straining ewe; easing the lamb forwards, front legs first, before it slips out, wet and warm, onto the clean straw. It's a heart-stopping moment, in the small hours, when you're briskly rubbing a lifeless lamb with a handful of straw, willing it to live. Left to their own devices, pregnant ewes have two peaks of giving birth – one just before dawn, the other just after sunset. Different sheep breeds show different preferences for either morning or evening twilight but

INTRODUCTION

despite hundreds of years of selective breeding and human interference, most sheep still prefer the half-light safety of twilight to both mate and give birth.

Many plants and insects are also drawn to dawn and dusk. To attract insects such as moths, who come out under the cover of dim light, many flowers have evolved irresistible twilight charms. Some, like the evening primrose, only bloom as the Sun sets, a twilight seduction while much of the garden sleeps. Others, such as honeysuckle, emit heady, intoxicating scents as daylight fades. Folk names such as the four o'clock flower or daisies (from day's eyes) often give away a plant's dusk and dawn habits more readily than any dry Latin titles.

There is also another twilight, one that few people know about, deep in the ocean. Known as the 'twilight zone', this is a place of such magical oddity that its creatures seem moulded from the stuff of childhood imagination. It is called the twilight zone because the animals who live there cope with light levels not dissimilar to late-evening crepuscular creatures on land, and they have had to come up with ingenious and sometimes shocking solutions to thrive in the darkest gloom. At dawn and dusk, an entire ecosystem in the ocean twilight zone also takes a remarkable, collective journey. It is a world breathtaking in its mad beauty and one, as we'll see in Chapter 5, that science is only just getting to grips with.

For thousands of years, humans have also been captivated by twilight's fluidity. It's neither day nor night, but a transitional time, when one world slips into the next. And, like so many things that refuse to obey convention, almost every aspect of twilight is strange and dreamlike. How we hear, see and feel things seems to change in the half-light. Sound carries differently in twilight; even perfumes travel further at dusk and dawn than in the day. Our ideas are also altered by twilight. Like that delicious point between sleep and waking, when the brain freewheels with unconnected but often brilliant thoughts, so too twilight invites different perspectives and ways of seeing. The word 'crepuscular' comes from the Latin for twilight, *crepusculum*, a word that probably itself emerged from *creperus*, meaning 'obscure'. Classical authors found the ambiguity of twilight a useful metaphor – *creperae* described doubtful issues. It's perhaps no wonder that so many of our folkloric tales and mythical beasts reside in the twilight – the boundary, or liminal zone, between the human realm and the supernatural. Liminal comes from the Latin *limen*, literally 'threshold', and in many cultures dawn and dusk were considered times when a portal between the spiritual world and ours opens up or becomes more permeable.

Twilight is truly the muse of the poet and painter. Artists and writers have, for centuries, tried to capture

INTRODUCTION

twilight's singular beauty. It is a preoccupation that seems to have almost disappeared in modern writing, but many of my most formative authors and books growing up - from D. H. Lawrence to the Brontës, *The Secret Garden* to *The Call of the Wild* - described twilight in its many different guises. Few writers, these days, spend so much energy attempting to use dusk and dawn as poetic metaphors or penning them as if they were characters in their own right. I have been accompanied by Charles Dickens's books my entire life, for example, and he was really good at using twilight to convey mood. And, in many cases, the kinds of dawns and dusks he described set the tone as vividly as any stage scenery: 'One beautiful evening,' he writes so evocatively in *Oliver Twist*, 'when the first shades of twilight were beginning to settle upon the earth, Oliver sat at this window, intent upon his books. He had been poring over them for some time; and, as the day had been uncommonly sultry, and he had exerted himself a great deal, it is no disparagement to the authors, whoever they may have been, to say, that gradually and by slow degrees, he fell asleep.' My own childhood was filled with those moments, of twilight naps in the back of our old car or deep armchairs, only for my father to scoop me up and, with the back-breaking love of a parent, lower me into my own bed before falling into a deeper, midnight sleep.

For thousands of years, many cultures from across the world have treated twilight with unique reverence, reserving certain rituals and observances for dawn and dusk. Mythologies grew to explain these events as gods and goddesses, heavenly beings who take the same journey day by day to bring us twilight. We even built monuments to celebrate special sunsets and sunrises, ones that still dominate the landscape today. At twilight, we waited and watched with awe.

And yet, I see a change. I am enormously lucky to live so connected to nature and abide by its rhythms. But the destruction of twilight is never far away. Few places, even in the countryside, are immune to the effects of light pollution and the modern world's insistence on being permanently lit. Shops, homes, streets, factories, even gardens – there seems to be an insatiable desire to illuminate absolutely everything, even when no-one's watching, turning night into an extension of the day. But where does that leave all the creatures and plants that need twilight to exist? Or use twilight as a signal that their day should begin or end? And what is that doing to us, a species that also relies heavily on these cues? In a time when so many of us live according to natural rhythms battered by artificial light, or spend most of our lives in indoor spaces that remove any connection with the sky, the need to hold on to the magic of twilight has never felt more urgent.

INTRODUCTION

It also turns out that writing about twilight, and trying to grasp its full meaning, is a challenge as shifting and tricksy as twilight itself. While it was easy to convey feelings about dusk and dawn in my diary entries from around the farm, I found remarkably few scholarly papers or books about the subject from recent years. It seems, as a society, we've stopped talking about the subtleties of the daily cycle - things either belong to the day or night. If you want to search the internet for any detailed information on twilight, you must first scroll through pages of vampire-fantasy thanks to Stephenie Meyer's wildly successful *Twilight* novels and screen adaptations. On a recent filming project, I was chatting to a young cameraman about writing this book about twilight, and he cheerfully asked if I was 'Team Edward or Team Jacob', a reference to the fandom debate about the novels' romantic leads. He looked crestfallen when I told him this book wasn't about vampires. Go back a century or so, however, and twilight is talked about continuously. History, poetry, drama, astronomy, nature writing, travel journals, agricultural almanacs, employment contracts - people noticed twilight and it mattered.

It seems as if the importance of this sublime section of the day has been casually eroded. Its meaning too - enchanting and ineffable - is fading before our very eyes. And so, this is a love letter. Or perhaps more accurately, an elegy, to twilight and all her fabulous secrets. But first, we start our journey in southern Spain, a thousand years back in time, with a man desperate to unravel the secrets of this peculiar time of day...

1

Rare Vapours, Rumbling Volcanoes and Simmer Dim

In the middle of the eleventh century, as a hazy Mediterranean sun sank below the horizon, a thoughtful scholar looked to the sky. Ibn Mu'adh was a polymath with an extraordinary brain. He spent much of his adult life trying to answer some of mathematics' most puzzling problems. He was obsessed with spheres and their trigonometry. And, far from being a strange and narrow field of study, Ibn Mu'adh's passions were directed towards all kinds of real-world problems – from how to navigate around the globe to the delicious riddles of astronomy.

Born around 1000 CE, in Jaén, a province in southern Spain then under Muslim rule, Ibn Mu'adh arrived into a world dizzy with learning. Now dubbed the 'Islamic Golden Age', the five hundred years between the eighth and thirteenth centuries were a period of intense scientific and cultural flourishing. As a young man, from a family of judges and legal experts, Ibn Mu'adh would have been exposed to a broad and rich academic environment. Mathematics, science and geography jostled for his attention alongside law, literature, history, art and theology. Debate flourished among people from diverse backgrounds, often prompted by new Arabic translations of ancient texts from other great civilisations who had gone before.

In the course of his work, Ibn Mu'adh spent hours observing the sky, poring over endless sunrises and sunsets. One particular part of the day, however, truly piqued his interest: twilight. For centuries, Muslim scholars had kept an eye on this special time; public calls to prayer were taken at morning and evening twilight, and sages spent hours computing complex tables that helped the faithful keep to their daily devotions. But Ibn Mu'adh wasn't interested in twilight as an aid to piety or a way of marking time. For him, twilight held the secret of the heavens. Or, perhaps more accurately, how high the heavens reached.

Contrary to what we're taught in school, plenty of thinkers in the ancient world believed the world was round. There were, of course, some significant clues. When a ship sailed over the horizon, its masts would still be visible even after the hull had disappeared from view. This suggested the vessel was sailing away over a gentle curve. During a lunar eclipse, the Earth casts a circular shadow on the Moon, something that wouldn't happen if the world was a different shape. Even the differing positions of the constellations, which shifted depending on where you were on the planet's surface, indicated that the Earth was a sphere. In fact, over a thousand years before Ibn Mu'adh was even born, the Greek astronomer Eratosthenes - using some basic trigonometry and brilliant lateral thinking - had already calculated the Earth's circumference.*

Ibn Mu'adh had a theory and wanted to test it. For him, twilight was a specific, measurable time between the moment the Sun disappeared below the horizon and complete darkness. Morning's twilight is the opposite. Ibn Mu'adh theorised that for the sky to be still gently lit, even though the Sun had dipped out of sight, the atmosphere was acting like a sort of mirror, bouncing the Sun's light back down towards Earth. The further the Sun dropped below the horizon, the higher in the atmosphere - or 'rare vapours' as he called it - its light was reflected. The very last visible rays of twilight just before full darkness, therefore, must be coming to Earth from the uppermost point of the atmosphere.

---

* The Earth is about 24,900 miles around the equator, slightly less around the poles.

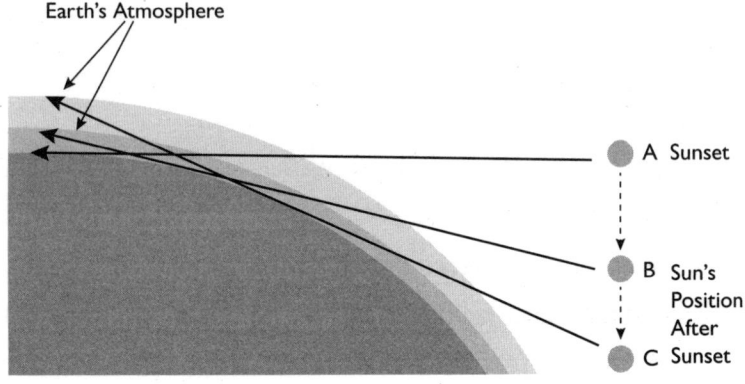

The ancient Greeks had already calculated that true night, when there is no residual sunlight, began when the Sun was about 18 or 19 degrees below the horizon. Their understanding of the celestial motions and ability to calculate time and angles allowed the ancient Greeks to make reasonably accurate estimates of twilight, even without modern instruments.

Ibn Mu'adh made a fantastically shrewd calculation, much of it based on information gleaned from these classical texts. Using simple right-angle triangles and the known radius of the Earth, Ibn Mu'adh estimated the height of the heavens. His approximation for the thickness of the atmosphere? About 52 miles high. Today, the boundary that separates the Earth's atmosphere and outer space is known as the Kármán line. It is not a hard, defined threshold but is generally agreed to encircle the globe at an altitude of somewhere between 50 and 62 miles above sea level. Ibn Mu'adh's thousand-year-old estimate, by that reckoning, was impressively accurate.

The truly amazing thing about Ibn Mu'adh's revelation, however, is that he chased questions about twilight not to please any great caliph or to answer a theological conundrum. Unlike many other scholars of his time, who toiled away to reconcile their faith with science, or earn the favour of those in power, Ibn Mu'adh did it because he simply wanted to know. Or, as in his own words, to 'relieve the inquirer of his inquiry and to add to the perspicacity of the perspicacious, to awake the slumberer from his sleep'.[1] Twilight had beguiled him.

Indeed, dusk and dawn still have the power to affect those who closely study the skies. There is poetry in stargazing. In 2010 Dr Martin Beech, a professor of astronomy at the University of Regina, wrote expressively of dusk and dawn in the *Journal of the Royal Astronomical Society of Canada*: 'A curse and a joy: these are the feelings brought on by twilight [...] there is science and discovery in those diaphanous glows – indeed, they tell us of the atmosphere.'[2] So too, Phil Platt, professional astronomer and science communicator in Virginia, North America. Of twilight, he mused: 'I have always loved twilight at dusk. The world quietens, and the sky itself heralds the coming of the stars. For an astronomer, twilight signals a welcoming to the universe, and the anticipation of that is one of the best things I know.'³

While Ibn Mu'adh's estimate was remarkably close, for centuries after people still understood very little about what the atmosphere's 'rare vapours' consisted of and how they interacted with sunlight to create twilight's colours. Argued over since antiquity, scholars knew that the atmosphere was a special place, where the theatre of water, wind and light played out. Nobody, however, could explain how the skies seemed to come alive with glowing, dazzling shades as the day slid into night, and back again. For that, it would take a handful of brilliant scientists and a bloody great bang.

Throughout 1883, a tiny volcanic island halfway between Java and Sumatra bubbled and boiled ominously. And then, on 27 August, it unleashed its fury. The eruption of Krakatoa is now known to have been one of the deadliest in world history, killing nearly 40,000 people and sending the climate into chaos. It also jettisoned billions of tonnes of dust, gas and debris 50 miles up into the Earth's atmosphere.

Within just a few days of the blast, people all over the world started to notice that the sky, after sunset, was an incredible kaleidoscope of colours. Beginning in Asia, and then spreading day by day, week by week, across the skies of North and South America, Africa and finally Europe, observers began to document remarkable and spectacularly vivid twilights. Newspapers printed hundreds of sightings from around the world. Everyone it seems – from country parson to college professor – was watching the skies with interest. Reports such as this, from a November edition of the *London Standard*, recorded the luminescent skies:

> the moment the sun's globe disappeared beneath the horizon, the fleecy clouds which hung in the almost transparent air became lighted up with a pink and then a deep red colour [...] every night the sky has been dyed in a wonderful glow of colour, leading the citizen unfamiliar with such a display in dreary November to imagine that some vast conflagration had burst out in the western suburbs.[4]

Writers, too, captured the scene, including Britain's own poet priest Gerard Manley Hopkins. He marvelled that the volcanic dust 'bathes the whole sky mistaken for the reflection of a great fire'[5] and that the colours are 'more like inflamed flesh than the lucid reds of ordinary sunsets'. Like a glorious colour wheel, Manley Hopkins's skies were awash with multiple hues: 'Above the green in turn appeared a red glow, broader and burlier in make,' he wrote, 'it was softly brindled, and in the ribs or bars the colour was rosier, in the channels where the blue of the sky shone through it was a mallow colour. Above this was a vague lilac.'[6] Alfred Lord Tennyson, who had also been gripped by Krakatoa fever, penned: 'Had the fierce ashes of some fiery peak Been hurl'd so high they ranged about the globe? For day by day, thro' many a blood-red eve.'[7]

Over in Chelsea, the landscape artist William Ascroft spent weeks trying to paint the sanguineous volcanic skies over London's River Thames, and produced hundreds upon hundreds of gorgeous, and now hardly known, colour sketches. Picking his way along riverbanks and field edges, pastels and board tucked under his arm, Ascroft captured twilight's extraordinary palette before it faded into the night. And, ever the artist, despite his sublime renditions, Ascroft felt he conveyed little of the event's true majesty. Later, he noted with frustration that his drawings 'could only secure [...] a kind of chromatic shorthand'[8] compared to the exuberance of the real thing. Some art historians have even suggested that Edvard Munch's 1893 painting *The Scream*, and his lesser known *Sick Mood at Sunset: Despair* painted a year earlier, were inspired by the unforgettable, graphic skies Munch had seen immediately after the Krakatoa explosion. Later, he described walking with friends near Oslo and seeing the intense twilights: 'Then it seemed as if a flaming sword of blood slashed through the heavens' vault - The air became like blood - with piercing strands of fire - The fjord - glared in cold blue - yellow and red colours - bloody red screeched - on the road - and on the railing - My friends' faces turned glaring yellow-white.'[9]

In January 1884, just six months after the eruption, the Royal Society set up a special committee to collate all the data, both scientific and anecdotal, that was being produced across the globe. In this early version of citizen science, the Royal Society sent out an appeal to the public for any information they had on the eruption's 'attendant phenomena'. Everyone from ships' captains to isolated missionaries sent in their first-hand, often vividly described, experiences of the volcano's aftermath. Others posted hastily done paintings, detailing the lurid colours of the evening's twilight.

One particularly interesting man also produced his own watercolours for the Krakatoa committee. German physicist Karl Johann Kiessling was a competent artist but an even better scientist and had become intrigued by Europe's unusual volcanic twilights. He was convinced the minute particles of dust and water vapour, which had been catapulted high into the atmosphere by the explosion, were causing the sky to put on an especially impressive display. To replicate the effect of the debris-filled skies, he built a chamber filled with gas into which he added small amounts of dust particles and water vapour and then shone a light through it, hoping to recreate some of twilight's colours.

Few were convinced that the fallout from a distant volcano could have painted the whole world's skies. John Ruskin, the renowned Arts and Crafts artist and writer, briefly wondered whether these 'unnatural and terrific' twilights might be due to what he called the 'plague-wind', a malign breeze filled with poisonous gases and soot from England's increasingly polluted factories. Kiessling's scientific hunch, however, had undoubtedly been inspired by another scientist's earlier work. In the 1860s, Irish physicist John Tyndall had conducted a number of experiments with intense light beams, shining them through various glass tubes filled with gases and liquids. Tyndall noticed that if you shone a light down the end of a tube filled with dusty smoke it appeared bluest nearer the light source and redder further down the tube. He wondered if this separation of light into its constituent colours could explain why, to the observer, the sky appeared to be different colours, at different times of the day, but wasn't sure exactly how or why it worked. What he did suspect, however, was that particles involved were probably so minute an entire sky's worth could fit in a snuff box.

Thanks to Kiessling, Tyndall and many other curious minds, we now know that the colours of the sky are created by a complex interaction of light and minute particles, and the eye of the observer. As we all learned in high school, sunlight appears white to the naked eye but is actually made up of all the colours of the rainbow, from red through to violet. At one end of the spectrum are long, red waves of light and at the other end, short bluer waves. There are also light waves we humans can't see – infrared and ultra-violet (UV) – beyond the opposite ends of this spectrum.

When these waves of sunlight first enter our atmosphere from space, they don't just pass straight through it. The atmosphere is made up of lots of infinitesimally tiny molecules of gases – mostly nitrogen and oxygen, but also other microscopic particles such as dust, water vapour and pollen – all of which create a pinball effect, pinging the light waves off in all different directions. Crucially, however, not all colours are scattered as easily as others. Short light waves, at the bluer end of the spectrum, are more readily scattered than the longer waves at the redder end. This is why the sky looks blue overhead.

When it comes to twilight, as the Sun sinks below the horizon its light must travel further through the atmosphere to reach the eye of an observer. This means that, by the time the sunlight reaches our vision, most of its blue light has been scattered away, leaving us to appreciate the glowing red and orange light waves of sunset and twilight.

Moreover, sunrise and sunset aren't quite twins; each has its own distinct character. Morning skies are often cleaner and clearer. As the day unfolds, shifting weather patterns and daytime heating stir up more particulates like pollen and dust, sending them into the air, allowing deeper reds and oranges to dominate the evening sky. These particles also have the effect of softening the light, casting a hazy veil over dusk. In summer, when the air is slower to move, this haze lingers longer, giving sunset a gentler, more muted glow.

What we learned from eruptions, such as that witnessed in 1883, has been invaluable in decoding how the sky appears to change colour during the day. We now also know that eruptions supercharge twilight. Large volcanic explosions pump huge amounts of sulphur dioxide high into the atmosphere, which then turn into tiny droplets of sulphuric acid and water. These scatter even more light, creating spectacular visual displays, and even have their own name – volcanic twilights. More recently, American journalist and backpacker Steve

Howe brilliantly described seeing the effects of the 1991 eruption of Mount Pinatubo in southeastern Asia:

> Experienced sunset watchers know that the more particulates present in the air, the better the light show. I remember a hiking trip through the Namib Desert of southern Africa while Mt. Pinatubo was erupting halfway around the globe in the Philippines. The volcanic ash and sulfurous gases that were belched high into the stratosphere filtered blue skylight into vermilion hues long before sunset. The atmosphere was so thick I could watch the sun without squinting as it sank like an egg yolk in tomato juice.[10]

One of the most remarkable things about the Krakatoa twilights was that people across the world described them in totally different ways. It's easy to imagine that dawn and dusk are the same, wherever you are in the world. And yet, as we'll see next, twilight is markedly different depending on where you call home.

In the early years of the eighth century, a quiet Northumbrian monk pondered the shape of the day. Alongside his monasterial duties, the Venerable Bede took a special interest in chronology, the science of time. The Church was keen that the Hebrew and Christian calendars should align, especially when it came to the holy day of Easter, and so Bede set to work trying to untangle the cycles of the Moon and Sun, months and days to get some clarity. In his later masterpiece, the *Ecclesiastical History of the English People*, Bede drew on some of these observations, including the special nature of British twilights:

> Because Britain lies almost under the North Pole, it has short nights in summer, so that often at midnight it is hard for those who are watching to say whether it is evening twilight or whether morning dawn has come [...] On the other hand the winter nights are also of great length, namely eighteen hours, doubtless because the Sun has then departed to the region of Africa. In summer too the nights are extremely short; so are the days in winter, each consisting of six standard equinoctial hours, while in Armenia, Macedonia, Italy and other countries in the same latitude the longest day or night consists of fifteen hours and the shortest of nine.[11]

While Bede made the same mistake as many other ancient thinkers, believing that our Earth was at the centre of the universe and the Sun orbited around us, it is fascinating that he mentioned different areas of the world had different day lengths. We now understand that how many hours of sunlight or darkness we experience depends on geographical location and the time of year – a variation caused by the tilt of the Earth's axis and its orbit around the Sun. Few of us realise, however, that the same rules also apply to twilight.

For at least three centuries, twilight has been categorised into three distinct phases: civil twilight, nautical twilight and astronomical twilight. The first – civil twilight – is the period of time between sunset and the Sun being 6 degrees below the horizon. To know what that means in layman's terms, at arm's length hold three fingers together, just below the horizon, and close one eye. That's about 6 degrees. Historically, in this period of early evening dusk the residual light in the sky was still bright enough for people to continue working or socialising outdoors, without the need for candles, oil lamps or rushlights (dried strips of reed dipped in tallow). Few of our ancestors would have been able to measure the exact angle of the Sun below the horizon, of course, so the end of the evening's civil twilight had to be marked by a more useful, everyday metric. For the educated few, civil twilight ended when the daylight was no longer 'sufficient to enable one to read newspaper print'.[12]

For everyday folk, however, the cut-off point was more practical. Civil twilight, at the close of day, ended when the light became too dim to do the most basic of outdoor tasks and you could see the first stars appear in the sky.

Charles Dickens described our shared daily experience of civil twilight in *The Haunted Man and The Ghost's Bargain*, the fifth and last of his wildly successful Christmas stories. Of dusk, he wrote:

> When it was just so dark, as that the forms of things were indistinct and big—but not wholly lost. When sitters by the fire began to see wild faces and figures [...] in the coals. When people in the streets bent down their heads and ran before the weather [...] When mariners at sea, outlying upon icy yards, were tossed and swung above the howling ocean dreadfully [...] When little readers of story-books, by the firelight, trembled [...] When, in rustic places, the last glimmering of daylight died away from the ends of avenues [...] When the mill stopped, the wheelwright and the blacksmith shut their workshops, the turnpike-gate closed, the plough and harrow were left lonely in the fields, the labourer and team went home, and the striking of the church clock had a deeper sound than at noon, and the churchyard wicket would be swung no more that night.[13]

It's interesting that Dickens mentioned 'mariners at sea' in his description of dusk. Sailors did indeed monitor civil twilight but also had their own, extra crepuscular window. After civil twilight ended and the Sun dipped even further below the horizon - between 6 and 12 degrees - those at sea enjoyed an additional 'nautical twilight'. For people on land, nautical twilight was as good as darkness. But, out on the ocean, this not-quite-night period was still useful. For thousands of years, ships have used celestial navigation to chart their journeys. In the daytime, they could use the position of the Sun relative to the horizon to determine their location on a wide, featureless ocean. Once the Sun had disappeared, however, stars became the points of reference. And, even though nautical twilight obscured most objects, there was still enough residual light to make out the horizon on the sea and plot a position - a sweet spot in the evening when it was dark enough to see the major constellations of the night sky but not so dark that you couldn't see the skyline.

After the Sun sinks more than 12 degrees below the horizon, twilight slips into its darkest phase - 'astronomical twilight'. This is the last gasp of dusk. Although it looks like all illumination has vanished, in reality there is still a whisper of residual sunlight, just enough to scupper anyone who wanted to see every

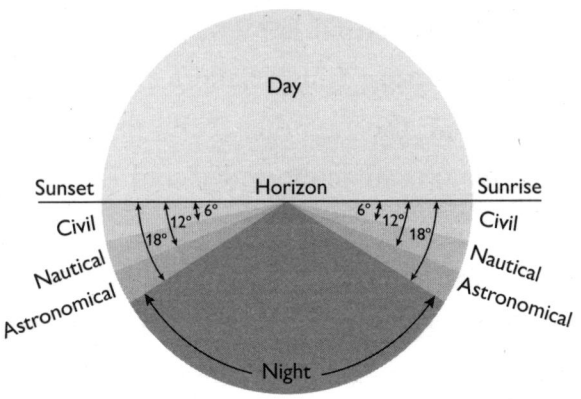

detail in the night sky. To the naked eye, most people can't tell the difference between astronomical twilight and true night, but astronomers (and plenty of organisms) can. And, while many stars and other celestial bodies are perfectly visible during this darkest phase of twilight, it's only during true night that the faintest stars and galaxies magically make themselves known. At dawn, everything happens in reverse. True night gradually brightens into astronomical twilight, followed by nautical twilight, civil twilight and then sunrise.

Far from being quaint, obsolete ways of describing dawn and dusk, the distinctions between civil, nautical and astronomical twilight still matter. In the UK, for example, a small but vital governmental department – HM Nautical Almanac Office – is charged with providing accurate times for the three twilights, at both ends of the day, for dozens of locations across the British Isles. This information, which is published online, is still hugely valuable to a surprising number of professions, including astronomers, mariners, aviators, the military, religious groups, calendar manufacturers, and even photographers and film crews.

Not all the world, however, experiences twilight in the same way. At the equator, where day and night are equal in length, regardless of the season, the three different phases of twilight – civil, nautical and astronomical – last little longer than about 20 minutes each. That means you've got about an hour between sunset and true night, and the same at dawn. The further you move away from the equator, however, the longer twilight lasts.

Twilight also varies depending on the season. In London, for example, which sits just over 51 degrees north of the equator, the three phases of twilight in winter last about two hours in total but in summer can stretch to four hours. In fact, between the end of May and the middle of July – when the time between sunset and sunrise is at its shortest – we don't ever dip into true night.

Here on our Yorkshire smallholding, for example, at the end of June this year the Sun set about 9.45 p.m. It was still light enough to see outside until civil twilight ended around 10.40 p.m., followed by nautical twilight that ended at one in the morning. Astronomical twilight lasted until 2.15 a.m., when it lifted back into nautical twilight, followed by civil twilight at 3.50 a.m. and sunrise at 4.40 in the morning. No true night to speak of, just seven barely illuminated hours of twilight.

In the first century, the Roman writer Tacitus wrote a book about his father-in-law. The eponymous work – *Agricola* – recounted the Roman general's experience of ancient Britain and its inhabitants. As is true today for many visitors to these islands, the weather proved to be a washout. And, for someone used to short Italian twilights, the dusks and dawns at some of Britain's highest latitudes were also rather surprising:

> Their sky is obscured by continual rain and cloud. Severity of cold is unknown. The days exceed in length those of our part of the world; the nights are bright, and in the extreme north so short that between sunlight and dawn you can perceive but a slight distinction. It is said that, if there are no clouds in the way, the splendour of the sun can be seen throughout the night, and that he does not rise and set, but only crosses the heavens.[14]

This effect is even more pronounced the further from the equator you get. The Shetland Islands, for example, are 10 degrees even further north than London. In the summer, for a period of two weeks the Sun never dips more than 6 degrees below the horizon. This means Shetlanders enjoy around 19 hours of full daylight and 5 hours of civil twilight but no nautical or astronomical twilight at all, and certainly no true night. This half-month of eerily illuminated evening skies has earned the ancient name of Simmer Dim, 'Summer's darkening'. Shetlanders have a knack for describing these strange weeks. Writer and native to the islands, Laurie Goodlad, recently described it as an 'interim period [that] gives a milky white light, soft and pure, bathing the landscape in a quiet, subdued cloak'.[15]

In midwinter on the Shetlands, by contrast, the shortest day consists of less than 6 hours of sunlight, and more than 18 hours of either twilight or true night. Exactly the same happens at the southern hemisphere's corresponding parallel, 60 degrees south of the equator – there's just no-one there to see it apart from the penguins. Only 10 per cent of the world's population live south of the equator and, Antarctic stations aside, there isn't a human settlement below 55 degrees south, a latitude and twilight scenario on a par with Newcastle upon Tyne or Copenhagen.

At the polar extremes, the North Pole and South Pole, twilight can last for weeks and weeks. In fact, for half

THE SECRET WORLD OF TWILIGHT

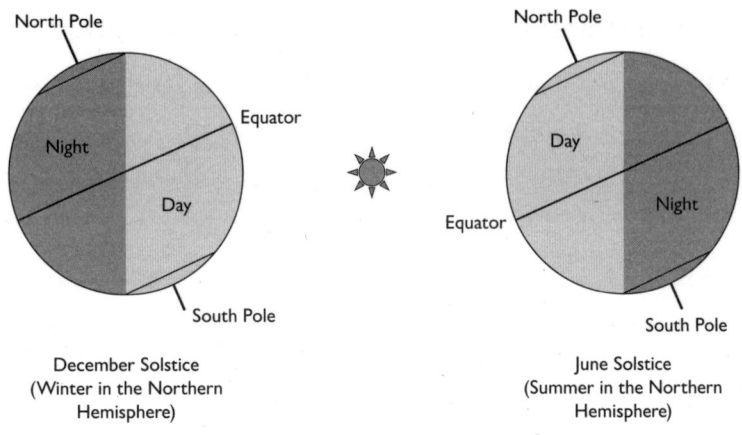

December Solstice
(Winter in the Northern Hemisphere)

June Solstice
(Summer in the Northern Hemisphere)

the year, the Sun never peeps above the horizon. And, although many people think of these long, gloomy months as constant darkness or 24-hour 'polar night', that's not strictly true. Only eleven weeks out of the six months of polar darkness are actually true night; the rest of the time is spent cycling through the three phases of twilight. As we'll see later, some of the animals and plants that survive at these polar extremes cling to these wisps of lingering light, however minuscule. For them, even the darkest of twilights provides just enough illumination to thrive.

So, we know that the duration of twilight can differ depending on the time of year and location. Which raises the question, 'Does twilight have any purpose beyond being a rather lovely, gentle transition from day to night?'

One of the most exciting things about twilight is that it turns out to be really rather important. In fact, without twilight, as we'll see in Chapter 2, nature's biological clock would soon start to malfunction.

Twilight Diary

Winter

It's been a spectacularly gloomy day. A brisk February morning on the farm can sometimes throw out sparklingly clear, ice-blue skies, but today has been nothing but wall-to-wall mizzle. It took two hours for the morning to lift from pitch black to sunrise around eight o'clock and, by the time the Sun had bothered to get up, I'd already checked the sheep and opened the coops, a job that always lifts the spirits. Both the chickens and ducks are always ravenous by sunrise and rush out of their huts, jostling for grain like Boxing Day bargain hunters. There's something strangely smug about feeling like you've beaten the sunrise and ticked off chores before the daylight truly kicks in. My dad, an inveterate early riser, always jokes that he's already been up and 'swept the dawn' when I ask him his plans for the day.

Ever the anxious smallholder, I take note of the changing temperatures as winter slowly defrosts into early spring. At midnight, last night, it was about 2 degrees but, when my alarm went off this morning at 6 a.m., it had dropped to zero. Yeats called this time the 'first cold gleam of day'[1] and country folklore has always insisted that the night is coldest at morning's twilight. It certainly feels that way. Even on a sunny dawn, when those first red-golden rays give the illusion of warmth, the thermometer tells a different story. Overnight, without the cordiality of the Sun, the fields and valley have slowly cooled. Just before sunrise, we've been in the dark for what feels like forever and the ground surface has lost most of its heat. Even when dawn has arrived, and the diffuse sunlight fills the sky, it takes a while for the chill to disappear.

When the sky is overcast, like today, there seems little discernible difference between morning, noon and afternoon. All day, the rooms in the farmhouse were a thin grey and shadowy, as if near evening time, and I was forced to put the light on in the barn to see what I was doing, despite its huge, open threshing doors. When it came time for the late-afternoon dog-walk, however, the day decided to put on a final hurrah. Looking to the west, the fug dissolved, leaving only a few wispy clouds just above the treeline. At about ten to five the Sun just dipped below the horizon and triggered the most ravishing twilight.

My walk took me along the edges of a neighbour's large stubble field. It's been raining heavily, on and off, since autumn last year. Deep ruts, left by tractors after autumn's harvest, have filled up with muddy water. The land is clay and acts like a pond liner, allowing these long, thin channels to remain waterlogged for weeks. The field looks desperate in the daytime – a touch of the First World War trenches – but this evening's dusk transformed the furrows into deep, tangerine pink zigzags, reflecting the fiery sky above. Just above the horizon, the sky was candle-red, with thin billows glowing yellow-hot from below. Rising upwards, the sky bled from oranges to pinks to periwinkle purples to a heavenly shaded blue – the blackened indigo of the evening sky is painted from an altogether different palette than the day's blues. The darkest shadows, however, were reserved for the ground. I remember once reading that darkness doesn't fall, it rises. Our hills, leafless woodland and clarted fields were almost black against the lighter, twilit sky.

Twilight's sounds often seem louder than in the day. Rural notes, ones that I don't ordinarily notice, somehow come to the fore. Dogs arguing in the next village, the excited shrieking of pigs, the reversing beeps of a cattle lorry turning in a farmyard – remote sounds suddenly feel eerily close. In this evening's dusk I could hear the mechanical hum of a distant tractor dragging a plough but the air was strangely free of nature noises. At twilight in spring and summer, the hedgerows and trees are full of squabbling birds, but in February it's silent, save for the odd startled blackbird. It was just me, the dog and drowsy twilight.

I find it telling that we have lost our ability to describe the subtleties of dusk and dawn or revel in their vernacular names. Most of us simply have no need to find words for twilight – it passes us by without any meaning or practical purpose. For centuries, however, people who lived and worked without the constant glow of artificial light would have been acutely aware of this special time of day and its nuances. Different regions had their own dreamy words for evening twilight. Many were riffs on a common word – dim, dusk or dag, the Old Norse for 'day'. Devon had dimsey, Somerset dimmet, Ireland talked about duskiss, while Dorset had duckies.

Other places made up their own terms, whimsical and imaginative in a way that often folk language is. Wales had its *cyfnos*, 'becoming night', Kent had 'boblight', from the Old English *bobben*, to cheat or deceive, while Lincolnshire enjoyed its 'darkling'. North Yorkshire called it 'clicking-time', the word 'click' meaning to shorten. Much of the north also used 'gloaming', a word often overused in cloying Victorian poetry. At first glance it seems a cousin of 'gloomy', too similar to be a coincidence. But it's much more evocative than that – gloaming comes from the Old English *glowan*, to shine or blaze like red-hot iron. My two particular favourites, however, are the south-west's 'creepy-crawly', a perfect phrase to capture the stealth of twilight, and the bawdy Sussex 'dragging-time', when 'the young fellows at fairs pull the wenches about'.[2]

And the Shetlanders, people who experience summer-long twilights, had more words than anyone. 'Riv' was morning's twilight; 'the riv of the dim', the first disappearance of darkness. The word probably came from the Old Norse *ryf*, to tear apart, so morning twilight was literally the rending of darkness.

(We also still use 'rive' in Yorkshire, to mean split into two.) Evening's twilight was 'mirknin', like the modern-day murky, and 'humin' meant 'the darkening air'. And the end of twilight, as it slipped into night, was 'dagset', the setting of the day.[3]

Dawn hasn't been quite so furnished with lyrical names but there are some lovely nuggets – creek of the day, peep o'day, cock leet, day-lightening, Aurora's harbinger, and dayspring. To 'daw' was a verb – 'Drink til the day be dawing' – and also meant to wake someone up. To 'dusken', was to make something darker or more obscure. And the word 'twilight'? Its etymology is as nebulous as the time of day itself. *Twi* or *twa* in Old English usually denoted two or double of something – we still see that in words such as twice, twin and twenty – so twilight may have meant the 'two lights', dawn and dusk. But it's interesting to see a similar-sounding word *tweo* in Anglo-Saxon meant doubtful or uncertain – for me, *tweon-leoht* seems more likely; a dubious, ambiguous time of day.

Walter de la Mare's 'Dream Song', a poem published in the early twentieth century, revels in all the subtleties of end-of-day light. Many of the phrases he uses – elf-light, taper-light, toad-light – are lost on the modern reader but would have resonated with readers used to the natural cues and ever-shifting nature of twilight:

> *Sunlight, moonlight,*
> *Twilight, starlight —*
> *Gloaming at the close of day,*
> *And an owl calling,*
> *Cool dews falling*
> *In a wood of oak and may.*
>
> *Lantern-light, taper-light,*
> *Torchlight, no-light:*
> *Darkness at the shut of day,*
> *And lions roaring,*
> *Their wrath pouring*
> *In wild waste places far away.*
>
> *Elf-light, bat-light,*
> *Touchwood-light and toad-light,*
> *And the sea a shimmering gloom of grey,*
> *And a small face smiling*
> *In a dream's beguiling*
> *In a world of wonders far away.*

I spend a lot of time thinking about people of the past. Almost every nook and cranny around the farm has traces of their presence: stone walls, heaved and knocked into place by hand; farm tracks, flattened by carters and horses; and old planted hedgerows, abandoned, that eventually ran riot and turned into unplanned, scraumy lines of native trees. I think mostly, however, of how people managed their daily routines, all the things that we now take for granted aided by alarm clocks and electricity.

There have been plenty of assumptions about how people's working lives changed over the last five hundred years, first with the widespread introduction of personal clocks and precise timekeeping, followed by the invention of gas and electric lighting. Historians often talk about a radical and crushing shift in people's lives; the emergence of urban, mechanised life must have marked a watershed, a point in time when our hours of labour went from the irregular, casual and unhurried to the regimented and minutely timed. Life before electricity, especially in winter, must have been up at dawn and bed at dusk, the fading light a signal that the day was done. Those who could afford to might have extended the evening with expensive candles or oil lamps, or not-so-costly rushlights, but even in the flickering light it was long assumed there was little to be practically achieved after sunset or before sunrise.

And yet, the truth is altogether different. In particular, it's interesting to discover how people told the time and what kinds of hours they did, indeed, keep. Diaries, court documents and other records from the fifteenth century onwards often contain critical information that tells us about the relationship of ordinary people to both time and work, and how folks measured the day. Until the eighteenth century, for example, few people would have had a timepiece. And, while middle-class families might have owned a house clock or pocket watch by the nineteenth century, it wasn't until the beginning of the twentieth that wristwatches became commonplace. For hundreds of years, therefore, telling the time for many people involved a much more intimate relationship with one's surroundings. Time was often heard and experienced, not read from the face of a dial. Parish churches would chime the hours, through day and night. The word 'clock' comes from the Medieval Latin *clocca*, meaning 'bell' – time was auditory. Records of people talking about time rarely mention minutes – time is measured in larger chunks of 'o'clocks' and 'half-hours', and they speak of events happening 'about' or 'between' these communally chimed units. This happened 'around half past six in the morning'; that happened 'between three and four o'clock'.

Folk, especially in rural communities, also seemed to have had an innate and surprisingly robust sense of time passing, with the position of the Sun and light levels serving as useful cues alongside, if you could hear them, village church bells. And, when it came to the shape of the working day, three key solar events served as fixed points – dawn, noon and dusk. The Elizabethan Statute of Artificers (1562), for example, dictated that labourers, who were hired and paid by the day, were expected to work from 'Twilight to Twilight' (civil twilight) during autumn and winter, while between the end of March and late September, working hours were 'from five in the Morning till seven at Night, from Lady-day til Michaelmas'.[4] These kinds of working hours were not only commonplace but sanctioned by law, well into the late nineteenth century, with punitive sanctions imposed on anyone who failed to keep hours.[5]

People must have used a blend of natural cues from dawn and dusk, and church chimes, to know when to leave the house for the fields or workshop and return home. Farmers' almanacs often printed tables that allowed employers to find the times for sunrise and sunset, and lengths of twilight, throughout the year. Time of day was also described by the use of lighting – 'candlelighting' was dusk and 'candle douting' (to dout was to put out a flame) marked dawn – a measure that seems wonderfully vague to modern audiences but was more meaningful to people who shared the same routines. So, far from being clueless, for hundreds of years people have had a good, if not completely precise, sense of what time it was.

They were, it seems, also entirely used to working, socialising and travelling outside of daylight hours and in light levels much lower than we could cope with today. Twilight required all our senses but it didn't prevent chores and leisure activities being performed in the half-light. From gathering firewood to spinning wool and knitting to feeding livestock, the day's tasks didn't stop just because the Sun decided to slip below the horizon. And, early in the morning, many similar dawn tasks were fulfilled before the Sun crept over the skyline. Over time, a detailed knowledge of one's house, village, fields, ditches and other local landmarks would have made journeying in low light easier, helped in no small part by all the other senses, including hearing, coming to the fore. I love the fact that in Yorkshire, 'to darken' meant to listen quietly or eavesdrop, as if listening intently in the twilight.[6]

In fact, the idea that people were only up and about between sunrise and sunset, in full daylight, is just simply not true. Historians of the early modern period suggest that a typical winter's day for a male servant or labourer, for instance, would involve rising before twilight and feeding the cows, clearing out the stables, grooming the horses, and watering and feeding the rest of the livestock, all before sunrise. A day of ploughing or similar work might end at sunset, around four o'clock in the afternoon, at which point it was back to the stables to repeat all the dawn's jobs. Supper was then taken, followed by an evening of chores – anything from mending shoes to sharpening tools, making cider to grinding malt – all done by hearth or flame-light. Even milking was done after sunset. A summer's day was equally long, with a greater focus on outdoor chores in the prolonged twilight such as mending walls, haymaking and digging ditches.

Children were also taught how to navigate twilight and run errands in the gloom. The 1748 parenting guide, *Dialogues on the Passions, Habits, and Affections Peculiar to Children*, advised small increments, to quash any fears of the dark, and a series of toughening-up exercises that might lead to bigger challenges: 'When you have brought them to be in the Dark without

Fear which Time will certainly bring about,' the author James Forrester advised, 'you must take the same Pains about Churches, dead Bodies, and the Tombs.'[7] An intriguing and early piece of research into children's fears, carried out by Stanford University in the nineteenth century, asked over two hundred and fifty youngsters between the ages of eight and fifteen what three things they were most scared of in a world. The results were then collated into different categories: ghosts, domestic animals (dogs, pigs, cows etc.), wild animals (bears, wolves etc.), robbers, snakes, the dark, nothing, and a deeply dubious category called 'common objects' that seems to have lumped together people of colour and drunkards. The results were both surprising and fascinating. The thing that most terrified children, strangely, was domestic animals, a category that won half of all the votes. By contrast, the thing that you'd most expect children to be scared of – ghosts – received only 6 per cent. As for the 'dark', that worried only 2 per cent, just nine children in total, and perhaps says something about how familiar youngsters were with living life in the shadows.[8]

*

One now defunct twilight phrase is particularly evocative – a 'blind man's holiday'. Its original sense, recorded as early as the sixteenth century, meant the end of the working day, when the light disappeared. But it soon came to mean something much more particular and expressive. It was the moment in the evening when, after sunset, the light had faded but it wasn't yet dark enough to justify lighting a candle – a sort of 'between lights'. For some, this ambiguous, dusky time was an opportunity for quiet reflection or, as one Victorian journalist put it: 'an hour of delicious idleness and sweet, sorrowless indolence'.[9] For others, regardless of wealth, there almost seems to have been a whiff of pride in seeing how long you could manage in poor light before lighting the candles. The satirist Jonathan Swift's 1745 *Directions to Servants* parodied the thrifty butler: 'to avoid burning daylight, and to save your master's candles, never bring them up till half an hour after it be dark, altho' they are called for never so often'.[10] A similar sentiment was echoed over a century later, in Elizabeth Gaskell's 1853 novel, *Cranford*. The character Mary Smith describes her host's reluctance to lighten the gloom:

Now Miss Matty Jenkyns was chary of candles. We had many devices to use as few as possible. In the winter afternoons she would sit knitting for two or three hours—she could do this in the dark, or by firelight—and when I asked if I might not ring for candles to finish stitching my wristbands, she told me to 'keep blind man's holiday'.[11]

And yet, there may have been a practical reason for also keeping a 'blind man's holiday'. The glow from candles and other weak sources of illumination was probably so minimal as to be practically lost unless deep darkness had fallen. A sharp contrast was needed between a dark room and its candle for any light to truly shine. Otherwise, as Jonathan Swift warned, you were 'burning daylight'.

While in English homes sitting in the evening's twilight seems more about parsimony and practicality than pleasure, in Scandinavian countries the notion of sitting in the gloaming had a comforting, contemplative bent.

Orvar Löfgren and Billy Ehn, from the University of Lund in Sweden, wrote about the Scandinavian experience and how strong variations in twilight have shaped its culture. In 'Daydreaming Between Dusk and Dawn' (2007), they note:

> An autumn evening in the 1930s a couple of young men were journeying through the countryside in Northern Sweden. Arriving at dusk to a lonely farmstead they found the door open and [...] saw the farm people gathered around the stove and in the red light from the dying embers. Nobody moved or said anything. Remembering the encounter with such a magic atmosphere, one of the men remarked: "It felt like a moment of devotion".

The boys had encountered a waning Nordic everyday habit of many names [...] "crouching in the dusk" or "keeping or catching the dusk".'[12]

Jan Garnert, a writer who has spent much of his academic life exploring the curious beauty of Nordic light and darkness, also says this about twilight: 'The dusk of the North consists of a liminal zone, a border zone, of light and darkness. Those who were able to used to enjoy a moment of relaxation in a "twilight sit"; the Swedish term (*kura skymning*) is one of several expressions for the habit of pausing in one's duties when it had become too murky to see, for a quiet talk, for relaxation in silence, or quite simply for meditative tranquillity.'[13] The same idea applies to Finland, a place geographically, historically and culturally intertwined with Sweden. In Peter Davidson's *The Idea of North* (2005), which explores the mythology and culture of far-north countries, he explains: 'There is an idea [in Finland] that it is good to sit in silence as the light goes, to observe nightfall as a time of contemplation – "*pitää hämärää*", "keeping the twilight".'

Returning to Yorkshire, on home turf, I particularly like Charlotte Brontë's relationship with twilight, one she would have viewed across the gritstone escarpments and lonely moorland of the Pennines. She seems to have regarded it as a dignified friend or spiritual companion: 'And Twilight to my lonely house a silent guest is come,' she wrote in her short poem 'The Autumn Day its Course Has Run':

> *In mask of gloom through every room she passes dusk and dumb,*
> *Her veil is spread, her shadow shed o'er stair and chamber void,*
> *And now I feel her presence steal even to my lone fireside,*
> *Sit silent Nun–sit there and be,*
> *Comrade and Confidant to me.*

Back to today's walk and I had just half an hour from sunset before it became too difficult to see with any clarity. Luckily, the dog and I had walked this route so many times we could do the circuit blindfolded. In the gloom, my black labrador Kip was just a silhouette and, at a distance, dissolved. In French, twilight was often known as *l'heure entre chien et loup*, 'the hour between dog and wolf', when one might be mistaken for the other. In Latin, too, it was *inter canem et lupum*. What a phrase to conjure up the image of a lonely shepherd, out on some unnamed hill, keeping an anxious eye on a flock. Pale-coloured sheep dogs have long been the pastoral worker's choice; even two thousand years ago, in the first century CE, Roman farmer and writer Columella noticed that the shepherds preferred a pure white dog, not only because 'wild beasts' were rarely that colour but also because it stopped the shepherd striking the dog by accident, as wolves often attacked at twilight.[14]

Safely back on our own fields, my near-invisible dog cheerfully sprinted off into the darkness, while I stuck tightly to the pale fence-line, making a straight path for the farmhouse's amber-lit windows. I passed the coops, all tightly shut and quiet. The hens fall almost instantly asleep and will stay in a deep, uninterrupted slumber until dawn but the ducks are always restless, even after twilight falls. They'll snooze but stay alert, often keeping one eye open. As I passed, they quacked softly but then decided it was probably nothing and settled down again for the evening.

2

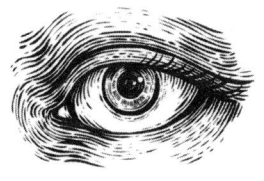

Zeitgebers, Blind Ducks and Seeing Ghosts

If you were an astronaut staring down at Earth from a space station, you'd see something quite magical. Called the 'terminator line', this is the constantly moving boundary that separates the half of Earth bathed in sunlight and its shadowy other side. And, far from being a hard, sharp demarcation, the Earth's terminator line is gloriously diffuse and fuzzy. This is twilight, viewed from the stars. It's a heavenly spectacle and only possible because of Earth's peculiar atmosphere.

By contrast, the Moon's atmosphere is pretty feeble. About ten thousand billion times less dense than Earth's, 'lunar air' is gossamer thin, with only small concentrations of molecules of helium, argon and a few other nebulous bits and bobs. This means that, when the Sun 'sets' on the Moon, day turns instantly into night. Here on Earth, the Moon's peculiar lack of twilight might seem irrelevant. Who cares if other planets have dusk and dawn? And yet, as scientists are just discovering, twilight may be one of the key reasons why life on Earth is possible at all.

Historically, scholars suspected that twilight was important because its gentle transition, from light to dark, softened the harsh contrast between day and night and prepared all kinds of creatures for darkness. In the middle of the eighteenth century, the German preacher Christoph Christian Sturm spoke for many when he explained the reason for twilight:

> To go all at once from broad day to dark night, would be very inconvenient. So sudden a change from light to darkness, would hurt the organs of sight, and might destroy them. Many travellers would lose their way, surprised with sudden night; and most birds would be in danger of perishing. The wise Author of nature has prevented all these inconveniencies, as by means of twilight we pass gently and gradually from day to night.[1]

While Christian was absolutely right to say that twilight is practically useful because it prevents creatures, including ourselves, being 'caught out' by the darkness, the relationship between twilight and the rest of the natural world turns out to be much more subtle and significant.

Most living organisms on Earth occupy a specific niche. This means they not only exploit a particular physical environment – land, water, air – but they also make the most of certain periods in the 24-hour day. As we've already learned, organisms who are busiest at night are called 'nocturnal', in the daylight 'diurnal', and those most active at dawn and dusk are 'crepuscular'. But the English language is a sucker for detail and so this word is further split into 'matutinal' (active at dawn) and 'vespertine' (busy at dusk). Some creatures and plants occupy more than one niche – some moths, for example, often emerge at dusk and will flit around, through the night, right up until dawn. Humans evolved to be both diurnal and crepuscular, depending on the time of year. From corals to big cats, toadstools to terrapins, different forms of life have their preferred 'time-slots' which help them avoid predators, find food, reduce competition over resources, avoid extremes of heat or cold, entice other beneficial organisms and so on.

To make sure an organism knows when it should clock-on and clock-off, it has evolved an internal biological timekeeper called a 'circadian rhythm' (*circadian* translates from Latin to 'about a day') that helps it stick to a 24-hour routine. These circadian clocks are found in cells of all kinds and, over the years, many experiments have shown that these rhythms are so ingrained that even when kept in total darkness, or constant daylight, an organism will still faithfully adhere to its routine for days, weeks, even months. Everything from hamsters to fruit flies have been put through their paces and shown to have an innate circadian rhythm.

There is, however, a rather important caveat to this. Circadian rhythms only run smoothly if they are calibrated against external cues. Just as a wristwatch often runs a little fast or a little slow, and needs to be tweaked, circadian rhythms must be regularly synchronised with what's happening in the outside world or they start to wander. To do this, organisms rely on external cues called 'zeitgebers' (from the German for 'time giver'). Many microorganisms and plants, for example, respond to temperature changes that happen throughout the day as a way of gauging what time it is (as a general rule, nights are cooler). Another zeitgeber is the Earth's magnetic field, which changes on a 24-hour cycle as the planet rotates on its axis. The most significant zeitgeber of all, however, is light. Moreover, two times of day are the most important zeitgebers of all – the two twilights.

We all sense that daylight changes throughout the day. Its brightness or intensity increases through the morning, peaks around midday, and then slowly slides back down into dusk. Light levels, however, also vary enormously depending on the weather. Light is measured in units called 'lux' (roughly speaking, one lux is the illuminance produced by one standard candle at a distance of one metre). A bright sunny day, at midday, can be 100,000 lux while an overcast day will be nearer 1,000 lux, a hundred times less bright. Twilight lux levels can vary hugely - sunset and the beginning of civil twilight on a clear day might start at 400 lux but end up around 3 lux as civil twilight melts into nautical twilight.

Even night-time can vary in terms of lux levels. While a full moon can still provide ¼ lux, an overcast moonless night sky barely registers $1/1000$ lux. Location can affect lux levels too: being underneath a thick forest canopy for example, or in deep shadow, can further reduce light levels at any time of day by 10-100 times. If organisms only used light intensity as a clue to what time of day it was, they'd soon get very confused.

And so, many organisms also monitor the spectral quality or 'colour' of light, which changes, in a predictable way, through a 24-hour period.[2] As we already know, although it appears white to our eyes, sunlight is made up of all the colours of the rainbow and different colours have different wavelengths. The Earth's atmosphere paints amazing spectacles with this palette, making the sky appear blue in the middle of the day and redder at sunset and sunrise.

At both twilights, the colour changes are at their most extraordinary. At sunset, for instance, the sky often turns a fiery orange-red and continues its ember glow until the Sun has dipped to around 4 degrees below the horizon. This is what's known by photographers and artists as 'Golden Hour', although its actual length in minutes will depend on time of year and latitude. As the Sun continues to fall further below the horizon, the sky's colours shift once again. When the Sun is between 4–8 degrees below the horizon, the ozone layer acts like a giant blue filter, its molecules absorbing the orange-red light, turning the sky a rich, purply blue before slipping into darkness. This ozone-blue is different, and a much deeper colour than a clear daytime sky-blue, and why part of twilight is known as the 'Blue Hour'. This dreamy dark twilight has inspired many a writer, including the Irish poet James Joyce. In his 1907 poem, *The Twilight Turns*, he writes:

The twilight turns from amethyst
To deep and deeper blue,
The lamp fills with a pale green glow
The trees of the avenue.

In France, it is known as *l'heure bleue*, a phrase made famous in 1912 when perfumier Jacques Guerlain created the eponymous fragrance after being inspired by a twilight walk along the Seine in Paris. While Guerlain may have coined the phrase and captured its scent, French Impressionists had long explored this peculiar cerulean light in their work. Monet's *Charing Cross Bridge* (1899), for example, captures a smeary London twilight using almost no other hue.

If the ozone layer didn't exist, twilight would be yellowish. As the Sun sets further, depending on the time of year and latitude, this inky blue twilight fades into night-time. The presence of clouds at twilight often highlights these colours, rather than obscures them, the dipped Sun illuminating them from below. Even on a dull, overcast day, the colour of the day changes in a predictable manner, albeit in a less dazzling way.[3] Organisms seem to integrate this information – both intensity and colour of light – to give them a sense of where in the day they are.

To understand just how important our circadian rhythms are, and how they are kept running on time by our exposure to daylight, look no further than experiments conducted by the French geologist Michel Siffre. Siffre wanted to explore how our sense of time was affected by being kept in the pitch dark for weeks on end. In July 1962, armed with a torchlight, he exiled himself to a cold, damp cave 130 metres under the French Alps. Without any natural light, calendars or clocks, Siffre tried to stick to his normal sleep/wake routine but increasingly found, without any access to outside cues, his sense of time started to wander. His diary recorded his disorientation:

> *[30th August 1962]*
> *Forty-second awakening.*
> *I cannot sleep tonight, so will give myself over to dictating in the darkness my thoughts on time and other things.*
> *I really seem to have no idea of the passage of time.*[4]

When he finally came back to the surface, eyes blinking in the blinding light, the press greeted him with great interest. What was it like being away from external cues? Did his body manage to keep time? Siffre had managed an extraordinary feat of endurance – 63 days in total isolation – and yet that was not how he had perceived it. When he emerged from the gloom, Siffre believed he'd only been underground for one month. In reality, he'd lived in the pitch black for almost two. Siffre also noticed other curious effects of being removed from day/night cues. While his body had stuck to a rough 24-hour rhythm for the first few weeks, it eventually began to wander. Days began to stretch out, time slowed down. 'Two seconds passed,' he later told a journalist, 'and I perceived it as one.'[5] Siffre also noticed that his memory was compromised in the darkness; if he didn't write things down immediately, he instantly forgot them.

Siffre's interest in time, and how our bodies cope with strange extremes, had been inspired by the frenzy of excitement that surrounded the space race. America and Russia were both busy catapulting its scientists into the cosmos, a place where day/night routines were difficult to maintain. Researchers had hoped that astronauts' natural 24-hour rhythms would continue in the absence of daylight cues but no-one had really tested whether that was true. Siffre's punishing underground experiment had shown that, while humans do indeed have an internal 24-hour circadian rhythm, it doesn't take long for it to drift.

Ten years later, in 1972, Siffre decided to put himself through it again. This time around, he spent six months underground in Midnight Cave, Texas. Technological advances meant that Siffre's physiological responses could be precisely monitored, while daily cognitive tests kept a close track of his mental state. By the end of the half-year ordeal, Siffre had not only lost all sense of time but also, temporarily, his sanity. Without the daily cues of sunrise and sunset, Siffre's sleep/wake cycle disintegrated after a month and his mind began to unravel. He contemplated suicide, found his hands stopped working properly, and began to struggle to string any cogent thoughts together.

He even tried to capture and befriend a mouse and accidentally killed it in the process. When Siffre emerged, he was a broken man. A deep depression, which had begun underground, stayed with him for months after he surfaced. His prolonged stay away from natural light also permanently ruined his eyesight.

Science is just beginning to understand how twilight – these two transitional times of the day – are central not only to circadian rhythms, i.e. daily cycles, but also 'circannual rhythms' or seasonal events. Many organisms monitor day length or 'photoperiod' to establish what time of year it is. In birds, for example, the arrival of longer days in spring triggers the growth of their reproductive organs in preparation for the breeding season. But day length on its own doesn't seem to be the only environmental cue that birds are sensing. Apart from at the equator, the duration of twilight reliably changes throughout the year and organisms seem to use its timings to regulate different seasonal behaviour. Everything from migration to breeding, moulting to feeding behaviours, is triggered by the yearly changes in the lengths of dawn and dusk. Plants and microorganisms are also heavily influenced by twilight. Which begs the obvious question: how do organisms, especially those without eyes, see it?

The fourth-century Greek philosopher Theophrastus wrote on an almost comically broad range of subjects. Clearly not someone who worried about being branded a jack-of-all-trades, master of none, he penned treatises on everything from bad smells to stones, sweat to weather signs. He was, however, particularly interested in plants. His two major works on botany – *Plant Explanations* and *Enquiry into Plants* – are now considered some of history's most important contributions to plant science.

Theophrastus is also credited with being the first person to note that plants seem to have some kind of daily rhythm, although he didn't have a name for it. Looking carefully at a tamarind tree, he noticed that its tiny leaves closed together at dusk but opened again at dawn. The same thing, he noticed, happened with rose petals. Plants, he remarked, seem to 'sense' the passing of the day. But how? To understand this, we need to know how organisms of all kinds – from tiny bacteria to blue whales – detect light.

As a human, with a pair of fully functioning eyes, it's tempting to imagine that organisms without conventional vision can't see anything. Most organisms, however, possess light-sensitive cells called photoreceptors. These amazing structures can sense and respond to the intensity and colour of light. In humans, these photoreceptors are in our eyes – in the retina – but in other organisms their location varies. In many plants, for example, photoreceptors are found throughout the leaves, petals and stems. The number of photoreceptors an organism has can also vary enormously - single-celled pond algae might have just a small cluster, while humans have over 100 million photoreceptors in each eye. Some organisms seem to be able to detect lots of different colours in the spectrum, others have a limited range.

In fact, science is fast discovering that lots of creatures, including reptiles, amphibians, fish and insects, possess eyes but also have an extra cluster of photoreceptors somewhere else in their bodies. Some birds, for example, don't just 'see' using their eyes. Many avian species have lightweight, very thin skulls that allow sunlight to penetrate directly into their brains' photoreceptors, which are located in the pineal gland. In other words, the birds can perceive changes in daylight with their heads. In a rather horrible experiment in the 1930s, a French neuroscientist, Jacques Benoit, showed that mallard ducks could still sense illumination and length of day even when deliberately blinded. If the blind ducks' heads were completely covered, however, they lost their ability to detect light.[6] Similarly, a cockerel that can't see will still crow at dawn.

At least one animal we know of can even dramatically change its vision to cope with twilight, depending on the season.[7] Arctic reindeer have eyes that switch from golden yellow in summer to deep blue in winter. Winter twilight in the Arctic is tinged a rich, purply blue, thanks to the filtering effects of ozone. When reindeers switch their eyes to 'winter mode', it makes them super-sensitive to blue and ultra-violet light. It's a unique ability (or at least no-one has yet identified it in other animals) and gives reindeer two key advantages in the long months of polar twilights. Lichen, the reindeers' favourite winter food source, reflects less blue than other colours so appears dark and easier to spot against the dazzling, white snow landscape. Wolf fur does the same, allowing reindeer to spot predators who also hunt in the half-light.

And what about humans? Ours eyes have two types of photoreceptors – rods and cones. Rods allow us to see things in low light, but aren't good at colour or fine detail. Cones, on the other hand, excel at colour and detail, but only really work in daylight. Rods and cones were also thought to be responsible for telling our bodies whether it was day or night and keeping our circadian rhythms in order. There was, nevertheless, a big problem with this theory. Some blind people struggle to sense what time of day it is, but plenty seem to have circadian rhythms that are perfectly in sync. This has long indicated that some other light-detecting process was at work.

A number of studies have looked into this conundrum, including one experiment in which a number of blind people were exposed to bright light for a period of 90 minutes. Tests showed that their brains, in response to the bright light, produced or suppressed certain hormones. And, while all the volunteers reported not being able to detect any light whatsoever, their brains were behaving as if it was sunrise. It seems that although rods and cones deal with vision, humans have a second group of photoreceptors at the back of the retina, ones that are nothing to do with sight but whose job it is to synchronise our body clocks. These light-sensing cells were first discovered in rats in 2002, at Brown University in Rhode Island, and subsequently identified in humans, by Oxford University, five years later.[8] These photoreceptors – which have been dubbed 'time of day sensors' – are particularly sensitive to the changes in the intensity and colour of light that happens around sunset and sunrise. They also tell the body to release certain hormones. At evening's twilight, they tell the body to produce the drowsy hormone, melatonin. And at dawn, they encourage the body to release cortisol and other hormones to jump start the day. Our eyes were therefore designed not only for perceiving objects, but for responding to twilight.

It has long been thought that the human skull, unlike a bird's, was too thick for light to penetrate it. A 2016 experiment in Finland, however, has challenged this long-held belief. In a series of tests, which shone light into the ear canals of live volunteers and into the skull of a cadaver, it seems that light can reach surprisingly far into our heads. And, because the human brain basically floats in a bath of clear, colourless cerebrospinal fluid, the research suggests that light shone into our ears might be able to reach parts of the brain capable of detecting light.[9] Further research is needed but, for now at least, there appears to be some evidence that we might be using our ears to 'see'.

It's also fascinating to discover that, although human vision is poor at true night compared to many other creatures, humans do seem to have eyesight that copes particularly well with twilight. A recent study by neuroscientists discovered that the human brain has evolved a special strategy for seeing at dusk and dawn. A team from Goethe University in Frankfurt, Germany, tested volunteers to see how well their vision worked at different times of the day[10] and used an MRI machine to scan their brain activity as the participants reacted to visual stimuli on a computer screen.

Our brains are constantly whirring away. While scientists have worked out what many of these electric signals do, there is a large amount of seemingly erratic electrical chatter that serves no obvious purpose. This background noise or 'brain static', as it is sometimes called, almost certainly has a useful function but we just haven't worked out what it is yet. The key point here, however, is that the brain is always busy and noisy.

At twilight, low light levels make it more difficult to see. To cope with this, it seems our bodies – driven by circadian rhythms – anticipate this problem and boost our visual detection at dusk and dawn by dampening down this 'static' in parts of the brain associated with vision. In other words, at twilight, the volunteers' eyesight was at its sharpest and could detect weak visual signals that it often missed in the fully lit part of the day. A good analogy might be to think of the brain as a noisy, crowded bar full of people talking. If someone in that bar needed to hear a specific noise, coming from outside, they'd need to tell the rest of the room to be quiet for a moment. That doesn't mean the room stops talking forever, just for the period of time when that one person needs to concentrate on hearing a specific noise.

Why we do this isn't known, but the Frankfurt researchers suspect that it is an evolutionary quirk that allowed our ancestors to sense and respond to danger. We humans are predominantly a day-dwelling or 'diurnal' species but our activities have always extended into dawn and dusk, when levels of light are significantly reduced. In our deep, primordial past, twilight was probably a particularly dangerous time, a period when humans would have been most at risk from apex predators. And, although in the modern world we don't have to worry about sabre-toothed cats or wolves lurking in the half-light, it seems our brain's twilight ability to look for them is still there.

If our eyesight is attuned to twilight, what about our other senses? The researchers at Goethe University also found, at twilight, a change in the brain's regions that deal with hearing and touch, suggesting these too might be heightened at dusk and/or dawn. Our sense of smell, for example, almost certainly peaks at evening's twilight. A study carried out by researchers at Brown University, Rhode Island, strongly suggests that the sensitivity of a person's sense of smell is linked to their circadian rhythm.[11] While all the participants in the study were found to have the weakest sensitivity to odour in the middle of the night, most volunteers' sense of smell improved just before bedtime. And, while researchers don't know why our noses are at their most perceptive at the end of the day, those leading the study suggested some curious possibilities. From an evolutionary standpoint, an acute sense of smell perhaps heightened our ability to detect threats just before finding a place to sleep. Or, it could have increased our ancestors' sensitivity to pheromones, hormones that encouraged us to forge social bonds, mate and nurture our loved ones as we huddled together in the evening.

As for our other senses, little has been proven but there are some tantalising bits of research that suggest both touch and hearing are also keen at the end of the day. Studies that have endlessly poked and prodded volunteers with pin pricks, electrical stimulation and other ways of testing skin sensitivity seem to indicate that our perception of touch is at its most impressive in the early evening. In other words, we are most in tune with our sense of touch not first thing in the morning, or night, or in the middle of the day, but at the close of the day.[12] [13] Scientists also suspect that our hearing, and certainly that of rodents, peaks and troughs in any 24-hour period and that certain cells in our ears respond differently to sounds depending on the time of day. Some studies suggest human hearing is at its most sensitive during evening twilight, shortly before bedtime.[14]

People who experience auditory hallucinations also tend to hear them in the evening twilight. One study, with patients suffering from schizophrenia, showed that three-quarters of all their auditory experiences happened between 6 p.m. and 9 p.m.[15] Ghostly visions and apparitions often seem to be reported at twilight and have been for hundreds of years. And, while it's often thought that these terrifying experiences are a result of our senses being somehow deprived and compromised, our imaginations filling in the blanks, it could be the exact opposite. It is perhaps because our senses, in the half-light, go into overdrive that we experience the fantastical. It's also not a new idea. John Dryden and Nathaniel Lee's 1679 play, *Oedipus*, chillingly captured this strange shift in perception from day to dusk:

> *When the sun sets, shadows that show'd at noon*
> *But small, appear most long and terrible:*
> *So when we think fate hovers o'er our heads,*
> *Our apprehensions shoot beyond all bounds:*
> *Owls, ravens, crickets, seem the watch of death;*
> *Nature's worst vermin scare her god-like sons;*
> *Echoes the very leavings of a voice,*
> *Grow babbling ghosts, and call us to our graves.*
> *Each mole-hill thought swells to a huge Olympus;*
> *While we fantastic dreamers heave and puff,*
> *And sweat with an imagination's weight*[16]

Back to my favourite, Charles Dickens; the master of twilight imaginings. Few authors have so vividly rendered the sensory experience of dusk, how it can turn familiar objects into nightmarish characters and set our imaginations racing:

> When twilight everywhere released the shadows, prisoned up all day, that now closed in and gathered like mustering swarms of ghosts. When they stood lowering, in corners of rooms, and frowned out from behind half-opened doors. When they had full possession of unoccupied apartments. When they danced upon the floors, and walls, and ceilings of inhabited chambers, while the fire was low, and withdrew like ebbing waters when it sprang into a blaze. When they fantastically mocked the shapes of household objects, making the nurse an ogress, the rocking-horse a monster, the wondering child, half-scared and half-amused, a stranger to itself,—the very tongs upon the hearth, a straddling giant with his arms a-kimbo, evidently smelling the blood of Englishmen, and wanting to grind people's bones to make his bread.[17]

Thomas Wharton Jones, an eminent Victorian ophthalmologist, wondered whether something might be going on in the eyes, in the dim light of twilight, which made people convinced they saw ghosts. A rather brilliant scientist with some slightly odd views (he pooh-poohed

Darwin's theory of evolution, for example, and thought little of procuring cadavers from the infamous body-snatchers Burke and Hare), Jones was intrigued by after-images in the eye, those impressions which remain on the retina even after the moment has passed; like writing your name in the air with a sparkler on Bonfire Night. Jones wrote a paper, for which he won a prize from the Royal Institution, about the eyes and twilight. He suggested that people who saw ghosts, dressed in white, usually did so at twilight. We now know these as 'negative after-images'. If you strain to stare at something for a long time, and then look away, you often see a negative version of the image floating in front of your eyes. Stare at a white circle and then look at a blank surface, for example, and you'll see a black circle. And vice versa. Jones's theory was that people at dusk or dawn were seeing white spectres after concentrating on darker objects in the dim light:

> In the twilight, a person, perhaps after having unconsciously rested his eyes on some dark object, such as a post, will, on looking towards the gray sky, see projected there a gigantic white image of the post. This, with a little assistance from the imagination, may be readily taken for a human figure dressed in white. Sensations being retained only for a short time after the impression has ceased, the supposed vision

of a human figure dressed in white soon vanishes, as visions and ghosts are said to do.[18]

There's an interesting trick you can do to test Jones's theory in action. Pears' Soap first printed this 'awe-inspiring but interesting illusion' – 'Yorick's Skull' – back in the early twentieth century. Stare at the X in the eye socket for at least 30 seconds and then look at a blank wall or piece of paper. You should see the ghostly apparition of a white skull floating in front of your eyes.

In 1592, an English warship sank just off the coast of Alderney, scuppered by its strong currents and perilous reefs. Nearly four hundred years later, in 1977, a local fisherman discovered this maritime graveyard, complete with many of the crew's trappings. From tobacco pipes to gaming pieces, muskets to cannons, the sea floor had preserved the contents of this formidable Elizabethan sailing vessel, including one particularly curious object. About the size and shape of a small bar of soap, it was a translucent block of Icelandic spar, a naturally occurring calcite crystal. It was also found not too far from a pair of navigation dividers, a compass-like tool that was used to measure the distance between two points on a nautical chart. Archaeologists and mariners, however, were excited. This innocuous lump of hard crystal might just be the only example of a mythical 'sunstone' ever discovered. Moreover, it had potentially uncovered the secrets of how the Vikings conquered the high seas without the aid of magnetic compasses.

The Vikings were famously skilled mariners, known to have reached North America nearly five hundred years before Columbus. They picked their ways across the waves using the Sun and stars, the swell and local landmarks as their guides but, spending prolonged periods in very northerly latitudes, their ships would have also experienced plenty of thick, cloudy skies, long polar winters and perpetual twilights. With direct observations of the Sun and stars impossible for weeks on end, it was long wondered how the Vikings got their bearings at sea. Only one clue, from a medieval Icelandic short story called *Rauðúlfs þáttr* (Red Wolf's Tale), suggested the use of a magical 'sunstone', an object that could determine the position of the Sun even in dense cloud or at twilight.

> The weather was thick and snowy as Sigurður had predicted. Then the king summoned Sigurður and Dagur (Rauðúlfur's sons) to him. The king made people look out and they could nowhere see a clear sky. Then he asked Sigurður to tell where the sun was at that time. He gave a clear assertion. Then the king made them fetch the solar stone and held it up and saw where light radiated from the stone and thus directly verified Sigurður's prediction.[19]

Experimental archaeologists and maritime historians have, since its discovery, looked deep into the idea of 'sunstones' and how they might have worked. It seems as if the crystal's material – Iceland spar – might hold the key to the story. This calcite mineral is transparent and has a rather wonderful quality – it can detect polarised light.

As we already know, the light that hurtles towards Earth from the Sun is made up of waves. Imagine holding a length of rope and flicking it up and down to produce a ripple – this is what one wave looks like. Beams of light are made up of countless numbers of these waves, but

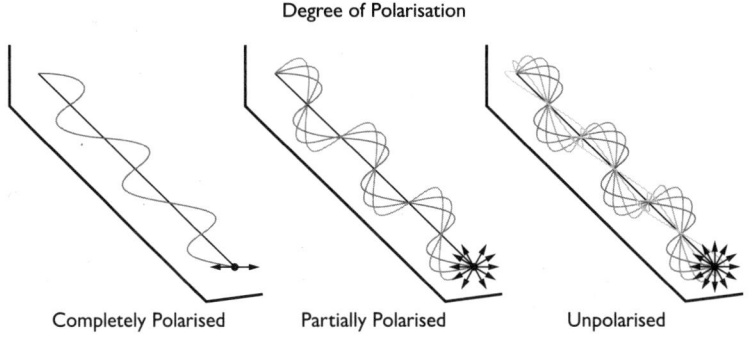

Degree of Polarisation

Completely Polarised   Partially Polarised   Unpolarised

they don't all oscillate at the same angle. Some wobble horizontally side to side, some wobble vertically up and down, and some wobble at any of the angles in between. This is called unpolarised light.

Polarised light, on the other hand, is when all the waves wobble at the same angle – think of waves travelling across the top of the ocean. Sunlight can become polarised if it's passed through a filter. Polarised sunglasses, for example, only allow light waves wobbling in a specific plane to pass through. Sunlight is also polarised as it passes through the filtering effects of our atmosphere.

Every year, science discovers new species of fish, crustaceans, beetles, insects and birds that can detect polarised light. What polarised light looks like, for each animal, might be different, but for some animals it seems they see a band, or bands of polarised light, at a 90-degree angle to the Sun. At dusk and dawn, this effect is at its most prominent, with a particularly noticeable north-south aligned band appearing overhead. Depending on latitude and time of year, for around 45 minutes after sunset and before sunrise this invisible guide is as good as a compass, revealing not only where north and south are, but also east and west. Being able to see polarised light is also an excellent tool for calibrating any of your other direction-finding senses. Dung beetles, for instance, use polarised light to keep moving in a perfectly straight line. Once a dung beetle has fashioned a perfect ball from animal poo, it must quickly roll it away to prevent it being stolen by another dung beetle. In a desert landscape, with very few visual cues, there's a real danger that the dung beetle – who is also pushing the ball backwards with its legs – could end up veering off course. And so, using polarised light as its compass, the dung beetle can steer its dung ball with confidence and speed. Birds also probably use the position of polarised light as an extra check when it comes to orientation. Before and during migration flights, they can bring together all the information they've gleaned from polarised light and combine it with signals from the Earth's magnetic field, daytime observations of the Sun, the position of certain stars and constellations, and recognising land shapes. It gives them, in effect, an extra sky map to steer by.

Remarkably, many humans can also perceive polarised light but are totally unaware that they possess this superpower. Polarised light produces an image in the eye called 'Haidinger's brushes', named after the Austrian physicist who discovered it in 1844. The visual effect is very subtle, and appears in the eye as a shape resembling a yellow bow tie, but it's actually one you can test for yourself. Open a blank white page on your computer or phone and stare at it intensely. Tilt your head from side to side and you might just see a faint yellow bow tie appear to move before your eyes. Most LCD screens emit polarised light to create a clearer, brighter image. If you can see Haidinger's brushes on a computer screen, there's a strong probability you'll be able to move up the next level of super-sensing and detect polarised light in the sky. This takes practice, but stand looking at a section of clear blue sky 90 degrees from the direction of the Sun. In other words, the Sun needs to be in line with one of your shoulders. After a minute or so, you might start to see a Haidinger's brush appear. Humans don't need to detect polarised light or, perhaps more accurately, it's not clear why some of us still have that residual ability. It's a wonderful mystery waiting to be solved.

So where does all this fit with the Viking sunstone? It seems that the unique optical qualities of Iceland spar, combined with the skill and experience of a Nordic mariner in using the crystal, may have allowed the wielder of the sunstone to locate the direction that sunlight was travelling from, even if the Sun itself couldn't be seen. Indeed, an experiment, published by the Royal Society, which used replica sunstones based on the Alderney shipwreck find, revealed that the stones could be used to determine the location of the Sun, even when the sky was far into twilight and the Sun was deep below the horizon. It was accurate to within 1 degree.[20]

It's easy to see why Viking sailors, in the absence of any knowledge of magnetic compasses, might have needed a sunstone, especially when travelling along high latitudes that experienced long winter twilights. But why did an Elizabethan ship, in the English Channel, need a navigational crystal when they would have almost certainly had a magnetic compass on board? Just as birds may employ a number of different navigational tools when they migrate, our Alderney ship might have been using a sunstone as an additional check. Iron objects, such as cannons, on a ship are notorious for creating something called 'magnetic deviation' – they can interfere with a compass's true reading. At the end of the sixteenth century, when the Alderney ship was afloat, the understanding of magnetic deviation was in its infancy. The sunstone, with its magical ability to detect the location of the Sun, even at twilight, could have been an invaluable instrument in any naval officer's chest.

Twilight Diary

Spring

In the middle of the night, our eldest daughter tapped on our bedroom door to tell us there was something rustling in her wastepaper basket. Go back to bed, we had both implored, it'll be nothing. After five minutes, she knocked again. The noise, she insisted, was not a figment of her imagination and it was definitely getting louder. Half-asleep, I staggered into her bedroom and headed over to the bin. Poking about among the crumpled envelopes and scraps of paper, expecting to find a spider or other wriggly insect causing all the fuss, I suddenly felt a rush of flapping towards my face. I screamed and staggered backwards, only to catch my foot on the back of my dressing gown and land in an undignified heap.

Sensing a moment of freedom, after being trapped in its wicker prison, a bat launched itself upwards and was now circling my daughter's bedroom like a stunt rider on a wall-of-death.

It had huge, elephantine ears and a wide wingspan, somewhere near the length of a school ruler. The poor creature must have been dazzled by the bedside lamp and was struggling to break free, whizzing around the bedroom in the hope that an exit might make itself known. Quickly, I threw open the sash window, flicked off my daughter's light, and the bat swooped confidently out into the dark.

I've had a few encounters with bats on the farm. Over the year, a handful have accidentally found themselves trapped inside the house but most tend to hang around the crumbling threshing barn, where there are plenty of nooks, crannies and broken roof tiles to roost. At dusk, from now in late spring, they come out in small swarms and become darting, almost swallow-like silhouettes across the sky. We have matchbox-small pipistrelles, who love to snooze in the gaps created when the linseed putty falls out around the barn's windows, and the occasional daubenton's bat skimming the pond. But I was thrilled to discover that our wastepaper basket visitor was, in fact, a brown long-eared bat, a species drawn to deciduous woodland and orchard, both habitats that we've taken great pains to plant here on the farm.

Between now and the end of summer, bats materialise as the half-light settles, a key window of opportunity when many day-flying predators have given up for the evening. The nature writer John Lewis-Stempel once perfectly noted, 'The day sky is cruelly riven by raptors', and the evening twilight offers safety and a generous platter of crepuscular insects. Different species of bats have their orderly roll call of appearance after sundown. Among the first to fly out here in Britain is the noctule bat, who can barely wait for the Sun to sink below the skyline. Soon to follow are the pipistrelle and the greater horseshoe, both often only 20 minutes or so into civil twilight, while species such as daubenton's and our brown long-eared bat seem to hold off and wait a full hour before heading out into the grey.

By staggering their starts, bats avoid competing with other bat species and, hopefully, time their emergence with that of their favourite insects. If prey is plentiful, bats will have two gluts of feeding – one or two hours at dusk and again at dawn – and will spend the rest of the night sleeping or mating, depending on the time of year. While many minibeasts are out and about during the day, plenty come out at night – in fact, globally, more insects are active under the cover of dim light than in the daytime.[1] Around the farm, as dusk falls, a salmagundi of bugs become available for bats – from earwigs to beetles, mosquitoes to woodlice – and a pipistrelle will demolish thousands of midges in just one night. One class of insects, however, trumps them all when it comes to the bat's dusk appetite: the moth.

On the farm, one of the finest is the gargantuan eyed hawkmoth. As caterpillars, they're fond of our apple and cherry trees and, once uncocooned and out on the wing, they tend to hang around these familiar food sources despite, rather cruelly, not being able to eat. Most hawkmoths greedily gobble up the pungent nectar of dusk-scented flowers, such as honeysuckle or jasmine, but the unfortunate eyed hawkmoth has swapped a working proboscis for super-sized wings and, as an adult, can imbibe nothing. Instead, it comes out under the cover of dusk just for a few, desperate days, hoping to mate. I occasionally find them hanging from the netting on the fruit cages, a rare opportunity to see such a grand and handsome moth up close. Moths are often viewed as the dowdy, dishwater cousins to our iridescent butterflies, but I find them just as prepossessing. In fact, often more so with their chunky velvety bodies and thick feathery antennae, the duffle coat and bobble hat of a creature that comes out in the chilly half-light. Eyed hawkmoths may look like crinkly brown leaves or a wobbly bit of bark from a distance, but any daytime predator that dares to approach, as the moth is resting, will see its wings open up further to reveal two hawkish blue 'eyes' and a flash of hot pink, a stark warning to keep one's distance.

The eyed hawkmoth and the brown long-eared bat are not that dissimilar in size, a quality that makes the latter's hunting of the former even more impressive. Unlike some British species of bats, which snatch tiny insects mid-flight, the brown long-eared bat aims its sights high and will tackle colossal moths which it then takes back to its roost to dismember. Hanging upside down, it'll chomp on an eyed hawkmoth like a corn on the cob, devouring its plump body and letting its papery wings fall to the ground. Often the only sign you're hosting a brown long-eared bat in a barn or outbuilding is the discovery of a ghostly collection of body-less wings, piled on the dusty floor.

A fellow North Yorkshire amateur naturalist, writing over a hundred years ago, was similarly smitten with the long-eared bat and tried to keep one as a pet. Lawson Thompson lived by the sea, at Saltburn, and was enthralled by a bat that regularly visited his entrance-hall each dusk in search of moths. The gaslit passage drew in the flying creature like a tractor-beam. Thompson, sensing an opportunity, captured the winged visitor and kept him in a cage in the hope of learning something revealing about such a misunderstood species. What started out as an aggressive prisoner who 'did not hesitate to bite' on any occasion, however, soon eased into something altogether more companionable. Thompson carefully fed the long-eared bat a diet of live moths, bluebottles and houseflies, which it speedily seized and devoured. He too noticed that the long-eared bat had no appetite for the wings of its prey and would discard them on the floor of its cage. After just two weeks the now tame bat was allowed out of its cage and given the freedom of the house. Thompson watched it hunt and flit around the rooms, hiding behind curtains and picking insects from the air. The bat also became so comfortable around its captor, that it would even take bugs directly from his hand. In the end, Thompson saw sense and gave the long-eared bat its freedom. Those few weeks of study, however, were probably one of the first times someone had tried to truly understand the crepuscular habits of a creature most people condemned as irredeemably wicked.[2]

For hundreds of years bats were associated with malign forces, spirits who were abroad in the twilight hours. The Bible wasn't a fan of the crepuscular bat, a creature that preferred the gloom to light, a symbol of spiritual darkness. The bat was also shorthand for anything furtive; as Francis Bacon moralised in 1625, 'Suspicions amongst thoughts are like bats amongst birds, they ever fly by twilight.' Rakish men were 'bats, who chase their twilight prey'.[3] Thought unable to tolerate the Sun, the bat was *vespertilio* in Latin, derived from 'evening twilight'. In ancient mythology, to be turned into a bat was a peculiarly cruel form of damnation; you were not only consigned to live in the shadows but forced to have a strange, translucent body and muted voice. In Ovid's *Metamorphoses*, King Minyas's daughters felt the wrath of the god Bacchus. At twilight, the 'borderland of light and uncertain night', the three sisters found their bodies changing into bats in the growing gloom as punishment for passing up the rites of the god in favour of their weaving:

a thin membrane stretches over their slender limbs, and delicate wings enfold their arms. The darkness prevents them knowing how they have lost their former shape. They do not rise on soft plumage, but lift themselves on semi-transparent wings, and trying to speak emit the tiniest squeak, as befits their bodies, and tell their grief in faint shrieks.[4]

The bat was also an animal confusing to early scholars, seeming neither bird nor rodent although sharing qualities of both. Such a liminal, category-defining creature wasn't fit for consumption, and regarded as 'unclean' according to dietary law – 'too much a bird, to be properly a mouse, and too much a mouse, to be properly a bird'.[5] It wasn't until the middle of the seventeenth century that bats were finally classified as a mammal, but that didn't prevent the body parts of these peaceful creatures being dropped into different kinds of 'cures', many of which aimed to steal some of bats' twilight abilities. From bat potions for improving vision in dim light to remedies that would keep you awake in the evening, the medical world was covetous of the bats' crepuscular traits. The thirteenth-century philosopher Albertus Magnus, for instance, was convinced that if you wanted to 'read books in a dark night, anoint your face with the blood of a bat'.[6] His contemporary and a Franciscan monk, Bartholomew the Englishman, recommended anointing one's eyelids with the bat blood to prevent any hair regrowing, a bizarre solution to surely an even stranger ailment.[7]

In East Yorkshire and many other regions, bats were long known as 'flitter-mice', a word that was also pilfered by our poet of the Krakatoa twilights, Alfred Lord Tennyson, in his 1880 'Voyage of Maeldune': 'Our voices were thinner and fainter than any flitter-mouse-shriek,' he wrote. Other folk names for the bat were also inspired by its dusk and dawn flutterings. The Anglo-Saxons called it the *hrére-mús*, the agitated mouse, a word that was still being used by Elizabethan writers five hundred years later. By then, it'd morphed into rere-mouse – to 'war with rere-mice for their leathern wings', Titania instructs her fairies in Shakespeare's *A Midsummer Night's Dream*, 'To make my small elves coats.' The Cornish called it the airy-mouse, while the Scots knew it as the backe or backie-bird, from the Old Norse *blaka*, 'to flap'.

In the early fourteenth century, Dante's *Inferno* cemented the association of the bat with destructive forces; the Devil himself was said to have wings 'No plumes had they, But were in texture like a bat.'[8] And Shakespeare threw bats into the cauldron of witchcraft, as evil ingredients in incantations and curses, none more so vivid than Macbeth's witches' 'Eye of newt, and toe of frog, wool of bat, and tongue of dog.' Vampires, too, could shapeshift into bats, a belief that has done great harm to conservation efforts ever since. In Bram Stoker's *Dracula*, the eponymous vampire would change into 'a great bat, which wheeled round—doubtless attracted by the light, although so dim—and every now and again struck the window with its wings',[9] but could only transform at dawn, noon and dusk. Vampires were also thought to be able to control crepuscular creatures – bats would do their evil bidding, but so too twilight-dwelling moths, owls, foxes and wolves. Even folklore had it in for the bat – bats in the house were almost universally bad luck and meant someone was going to die imminently.

One of the most ridiculous pieces of folklore about bats was that women shouldn't go out at dusk or they would almost certainly get a bat tangled in their hair. In fact, bats were said to be so attracted to female hair in twilight that they would get lethally ensnared and the only way to remove them was to have all one's tresses cut off. No doubt designed to control women from venturing out in the evenings, the folklore proved so influential that it was still bandied around in the 1950s. Rather tired of the rumour, the eminent conservationist Gathorne Gathorne-Hardy, who also happened to be the Earl of Cranbrook, performed a wonderfully eccentric experiment. Writing about it later in the 'Notes & Observations' section of *The Transactions of the Suffolk Naturalists' Society*, he cheerfully recorded:

> A newly caught pipistrelle [...] struggling, squeaking and biting, was pushed into the fairly long curly hair at the back of the head of a brunette in the middle 30's. The bat climbed with care up onto the crown of the victim's head and took flight without getting entangled in any way. Suffolk Naturalists can take a vicarious pride in the fact that three Suffolk women have been found [...] ready to test the truth of a hoary superstition.[10]

In fact, Gathorne-Hardy managed to find four more species of bats to stuff into women's hair – a noctule, a long-eared, a natterer's and a daubenton's – and, needless to say, every time the experiment was repeated the bats had no difficulty navigating the volunteers' heads and took flight without issue.

Keen to get a fuller picture, Gathorne-Hardy added his hope for further research: 'it is to be hoped that some brave West Country women will try with the horseshoe bats (*Rhinolophus*, sp.), which are not available in Suffolk'. It's not clear whether anyone stepped forward.

The evolutionary battle for twilight survival between bats and moths has been a persistent nuclear arms race. Antipredator adaptations are met with predator counter-adaptations, a cycle of escalation that has been raging for millions of years. Bats developed echolocation, moths evolved ways of hearing it; bats responded with calls outside the range of moths' hearing, moths discovered a method of jamming echolocation signals. Particularly fluffy moths, for example, are wearing a kind of acoustic camouflage jacket, their fur absorbing most of the ultrasound waves coming their way. Some species of hawkmoths even rub their genitals against their abdomen to produce a high-pitched squeak that keeps crepuscular bats at bay. More on twilight singing penises later.

One of the most amazing things about bats, however, is just how well adapted they are to twilight, a niche that they may have been forced to inhabit against their will. Evolutionary studies suggest that birds probably pressured bats to move from being day-dwelling creatures to tenants of the evening and early hours. Roughly 50 million years ago, bats may have been pushed into twilight by competition from other insect-eating birds and, perhaps more importantly, predatory birds with an appetite for bats. They have, however, mastered their metier and developed remarkable skills. Not only have they honed echolocation, where high-frequency sonar is used to locate objects in their environment, but many bats have also evolved eyesight perfectly suited to dusk and dawn. The idiom 'blind as a bat' simply isn't true. Bats' eyes are packed full of photoreceptors that work well in low light (most bats have between two to four times as many rods as the human eye), and plenty of bat species seem to be capable of also seeing some colours and UV light in conditions we would see as darkness. Flying at evening twilight, where levels of light vary as dusk slips into night, bats seem to be able to use both senses – vision and echolocation – to navigate their world with ease. Some species of bat also appear to be super-smellers, using scent to entice their partners in the half-light, a time of day that we already know is ideal for transmitting strong odours. The male South American sac-winged bat, for example, at dawn and dusk, uses his wing to waft a fabulously potent perfume blended from urine, saliva and penile secretions over the female. It's deeply seductive, apparently.

My vegetable and flower garden, at dusk, is so sweetly scented it must be hard for a moth or any other crepuscular insect to fight its charms. There are some obvious show-offs — the honeysuckle, nicotiana and jasmine — but there are other less well-known plants that smell heavenly after the Sun sets. The broad beans in the raised beds, for example, have remarkably scented flowers, candy sweet and vanilla-like, and if our valley is planted with acres of their smaller cousin, field beans, the early evening June air hums with the most sublime perfume.

Other flowers dotted in the lawn — buttercups, dandelions and daisies — change their shape at twilight — closing their petals until dawn as if shutting up shop. In fact, a stroll around the garden near the end of civil dusk, when the light has nearly disappeared, can be disquieting as a number of plants seem to wilt after sunset. Lupin leaves, which are stiffly star-burst during the day, droop at twilight. Runner bean seedlings flop their leaves, like a bird drooping its wings by its side, a behaviour that in warmer climes can also be seen in soy beans. A kitchen gardener I know tells me the leaves of her courgettes, squashes and some varieties of lettuce also slowly move at the darkening of the evening.

As a child I pored over Cicely Mary Barker's *Flower Fairies* and read her books as fact, not fiction. Each flower had a fairy, one that embodied the plant's character and idiosyncrasies. I longed for the garden's sprites and nymphs to be real, and become my friends, but as an adult I now see that Barker's true gift was to teach children about plants and their unique traits. My flea-like attention span was especially held by descriptions of floral pixies that came alive after bedtime: the jasmine fairy, who gives fragrance to the night 'as twilight deepens', or the dianthus fairy who, at dawn, snipped the edges of the petals with her pinking shears. There was also a tangible sense that the garden, the woodland and the waysides were full of life, even after sunset: the elves bedding down in fluffy old man's beard; fairies using the candle-like Lords and Ladies to guide them home from the evening dance; or the bugle fairy, keeping night watch on the scrub fringes of the woodland.

While Cicely Mary Barker's inter-war world was one of child-like innocence and kindly sprites, for centuries folklore had viewed fairies as cryptic tricksters, supernatural beings that were neither entirely good nor completely wicked. Seventeenth-century minister and folklore scholar, Robert Kirk, famously recorded the supernatural beliefs of Scottish rural communities. Of fairies, they were thought to be of a 'middle nature'. This meant somewhere 'between man and angel', morally ambiguous but highly intelligent. Crucially, such in-between beings were 'best seen in twilight', their bodies – like the light at dawn and dusk – changeable, fluid and apt to disappear.[11] Few at the time would have thought Kirk's ideas outlandish, however, as fairies had long been thought to inhabit dusk and dawn. Nearly a century earlier, William Browne had celebrated rural life and nature in his epic poem *Britannia's Pastorals*. In it, he talked of 'A Hillocke rise, where oft the Fairy-Queene, At twylight sate, and did command her Elves'; Shakespeare famously featured an entire cast of magical forest fairies in *A Midsummer Night's Dream*, who, along with ghosts and damned spirits, disappeared into thin air at the first glint of 'Aurora's harbinger', the morning's dawn.

In Celtic mythology, twilight was a time when the boundaries between the human world and the Otherworld, with all its strange fairy inhabitants, became porous. Accounts of this supernatural place, one that sat in uncomfortable proximity to the real world, differently located the Otherworld as below the ground, in a cave, up in the sky, or on a remote island, but a shared trait among them all was that the barrier between the two worlds became thinner, more permeable, at certain liminal times. Fairies might leap through the barrier but mortals may also be pulled into Otherworld. In Walter Scott's 1810 poem, 'The Lady of the Lake', which drew on established Scottish folklore, we learn: 'It was between the night and day, When the Fairy King has power, That I sunk down in a sinful fray, And, 'twixt life and death, was snatch'd away To the joyless Elfin bower.' It was an idea as old as time – the ancient Greeks had understood twilight as a time when the gods might reveal themselves to mortals. 'When the light of the sun fades, and twilight falls upon the earth,' wrote the Greek poet Pindar, 'The gods watch over us, and the stars reveal their secret.'

French mythology, much of it derived from Celtic tales, also conjured up Dames Blanches or white ladies, female spirits who floated around caves and ravines. Half-light hid these shapeshifting beings, who vexed travellers with their mischievous demands. They 'come only at twilight', wrote one nineteenth-century folklorist, 'as if evoked from a silvery stream, and disappear as if by enchantment among the floating mists'. Their 'pale, shadowy form', he continued, 'may be seen gliding gently along at the witching hour'.[12] The Dames Blanches typically forced passers-by to curtsy or dance, harangued by the white ladies' crepuscular companions – cats, owls and lutins, mischievous elves who also lived in the dawn and dusk shadows. The French and Swiss mountains were also haunted by the Cheval Gauvin, who galloped along valley bottoms in twilight, killing anyone who tried to ride it. A similar half-light horse appears in Irish folklore, the Pouke or Phooka. Pretending to be tame, the Phooka would let the unwitting climb on its back only to gallop madly away, taking the unlucky rider to their death before the sunrise.

The idea of goblins, sprites and fairies flitting around a dusky garden may have been inspired by two of our most magical crepuscular creatures – fireflies and glow-worms. Misnamed – both are in fact beetles – these ethereal insects seem to prefer twilight to any other time. Memories from childhood holidays, dawdling around rural northern Italy in an old caravan, often return to early evening walks along farm tracks and meadow margins. There, I'd see fireflies whip across the sky, in ones and twos, like sparks from a grinding wheel.

A male firefly will whizz through the air at the first sign of dusk. His body flashes, in a pattern specific only to his species, in the hope of finding a mate in the dying light. If a female sees his display, she'll flash back the same sequence – two abdomens, blinking like pixie lanterns in the darkening. Some female fireflies are undercover murderesses, however, and will lure the male of a different species to his death. At twilight, she'll flash as if she's a compatible lover, only to kill and eat the unsuspecting male who answers her call.

In Britain, we don't have the firefly, only its sedate relative, the ground-dwelling glow-worm, who sparkles from hedgerows and grassland. Hiding under the soil or a damp log during the day, the female *Lampyris noctiluca*, or 'night lamp', ventures out at twilight during summer and switches on her light. Nineteenth-century writers, surprisingly, knew only the female glowed, but the 'why' was more difficult to explain: 'It is the lady,' suggested one nineteenth-century journal, 'who, when soft twilight spreads over the dewy woods and fields, lights her pale, emerald lamp among the grass; that her wandering spouse, or truant lover, may know where she is.' Unlike the firefly, who blinks on and off, the glow-worm will gently radiate for a couple of hours after sunset, take her night rest, and then spark up again just before sunrise. In Shakespeare's *Hamlet*, the glow-worm's illumination was a sign that early dawn was imminent; the Ghost warned 'The glow-worm shows the matin to be near, And gins to pale his uneffectual fire', a wonderful observation that, unfortunately, misgendered its subject. The glow-worm was also the subject of tall tales, stories of weary travellers being led to safety by armies of tiny lustrous lights or vicars reading twilight sermons by the light of a glow-worm. Even First World War trenches were said to be gently illuminated by jars of glow-worms, collected by soldiers with no other means of reading maps or letters, although it would have taken thousands to produce the same light as just one single candleflame.

Species of fireflies and glow-worms put on a light show to attract mates or signal to predators that they're toxic. They produce their radiance using a chemical reaction in their own bodies, a magical ability called 'bioluminescence'. For all their fairy-light beauty, however, their bioluminescent displays are easily masked by natural light. Both daylight and moonlight can interfere with their urge to glow and so the crepuscular hours seem to provide the perfect backdrop for a bioluminescent show.

Glow-worms were sometimes even mistaken for 'corpse candles', mysterious dusk lights that were said to flit around the home of someone fated to die, or congregate at the side of a haunted road. One wonderful tale from the 1880s, recounted in the parlour-room favourite, *The Gentleman's Magazine*, entertained readers with a West Sussex household sent into a panic when a tiny pale light was seen 'to move over the bed of a sick person and, after flickering for some time in different parts of the room, vanish through the window'.[13] The bedridden patient was terrified at the dreadful appearance of the 'corpse candle', only to discover later that evening, that the tiny, ghostly light which had dropped onto her open book and lit up the pages, was just a harmless glow-worm.

Under the cover of dusk, I've noticed that snails and slugs also head out into my garden, emerging from their day-time boltholes. Only a few of them will nibble the cabbages and salad leaves, however; most do much more important heavy lifting in the vegetable plot, chomping through dead material, clearing up animal dung and carrion, and even eating other insects and gastropods. They're my twilight recyclers. If I accidentally lift a plant pot, or open the compost bin, any slugs or snails hiding inside will recoil in the bright light and instantly move to a shadier crevice. Dusk creatures like these seem especially misunderstood; we assume we know what they do, even if we've never bothered to look. Most gardening advice has failed to move on from the likes of Violet Purton Biddle, an Edwardian gardener whose otherwise charming books insist that 'The best garden as a rule has the fewest insects', and recommends a vigorous twilight assault on slugs armed with a pointed stick, some salt and a pail of water.

A gastropod's slimy, glittering trail takes a huge amount of energy to produce but, without it, the creature would be lost in the gloom. Like Hansel and Gretel, deep in the woods, snails and slugs use their silvery tracks to help them retrace their movements, back to their small patch of territory under a plant pot or in a damp crevice, after an evening's outings. It takes about a third of a gastropod's calorie intake to produce its mucus trail. Some very canny snails and slugs cheat and follow the trail of a fellow gastropod that lives nearby, piggybacking on their efforts. The dusk vegetable bed is a super-highway of glistening threads, directing its miniature passengers, albeit at a snail's pace, from home to food to back home again.

Even in temperate Yorkshire, a warm summer's day can be too much for an insect at risk from crisping up in the glare of the Sun. Woodlice, millipedes and centipedes all share a similar problem and have a cuticle (outer layer) that is neither waxy nor water-resistant. In the sunlight, they lose water rapidly, so will hide in a moist, dark corner during the day. But, as twilight falls and the temperature cools, they'll start to rouse.

Earthworms also begin to emerge at dusk. As light levels fall, the deep-burrowing earthworm (the biggest garden worm, fat and long like a pencil) will venture slowly upwards from the soil's depths, to spend from dusk to dawn finding rotting vegetation on the surface and dragging it back into its subterranean lair. Deep-burrowing earthworms also only mate on the surface of the soil, a long and protracted entwinement that can only happen out of the glare of drying daylight. The arrival of dusk even gives the earthworm's intelligence a boost. Earthworms have, in past experiments, been 'taught' to navigate through simple mazes by the rather horrible method of giving them electric shocks if they go the wrong way. Remarkably, earthworms remember the unpleasant sensation and, when they're made to follow the maze a second, third, fourth time, will eventually learn how to get through unscathed. The time of day the experiment takes place affects how quickly an earthworm will learn – day learning is much slower than learning that happens between dusk and dawn.[14]

It's perhaps fortunate that earthworms are at their smartest after sunset, as that's when one of their greatest gourmands also emerges. Hedgehogs are one of our most endangered twilight creatures, and spring is the time when they'll begin recovering from their winter hibernation. After months of surviving on fat reserves and fresh air, hedgehogs are almost insatiable in their appetites for garden insects and carrion, and will head out straight after sunset and continue their foraging through to sunrise. Snuffling and secretive, the hedgehog has, like many creatures of twilight, become a focus for suspicion and accusations of evil intent. Hedgehogs were once thought to be sorceresses, shapeshifted, a disguise that meant it was prudent to destroy any hedgehog that crossed one's path. Shakespeare's witches, in *Macbeth*, famously include the 'hedge-pig' in their 'Double, double toil and trouble' spell, and during England's seventeenth-century witchcraft trials, one woman described the

Devil appearing to her as a hedgehog, at the crack of dawn, and suckling her left breast. Twilight milk-stealing, from human or otherwise, has long been the alleged crime of the hedgehog, despite this shy, industrious creature remaining resolutely lactose intolerant. For the hedgehog, being a dusk and dawn dweller hasn't protected it from harm but has, instead, blurred fact and fiction. Despite being rarely seen or heard, hedgehogs have been wrongly blamed for crepuscular crimes such as eating young game-birds, stealing apples and thieving hens' eggs, all under the cover of half-light.

Only in Victorian times did the hedgehog enjoy a brief window of appreciation for its ability to hoover up the vermin that infested squalid urban dwellings. The 1862 *Hand-book About Our Domestic Pets* praised the domestic use of the hedgehog, a night-cleaner who if 'treated generously and kindly' would work its magic after the Sun had set. It was easy to procure a captive hedgehog at a local city market for a few pence, the supply constantly replenished – at least between spring and autumn – from the surrounding countryside. Taken home and given a few kitchen cloths for its day bed, the hedgehog would then be encouraged to roam freely around the dwelling from dusk until dawn, munching on infestations of black-beetles and cockroaches, as well as attacking mice and rats. 'Roaming about the kitchen at night,' instructed the helpful guide, 'this diminutive creature makes great noises, and will even lift aside heavy saucepans in pursuit of its prey.'[15] Magazines and pet manuals were still handing out advice on the best way to keep a pet hedgehog, for twilight pest control, well into the 1920s.

Even domestic cats have a preference for twilight. As a child, I had a succession of half-feral moggies who, despite being doted upon and generously fed, all retained their cloak-and-dagger tendencies. One, a black and white stray called Meg, would always sleep at the foot of my bed. She'd come and go silently through the night, curling up between my ankles for sporadic naps, but always be gone before sunrise, leaving a warm, slightly muddy hollow in the covers. Elizabeth Barrett Browning must have experienced the same. Her 1836 poem, 'The Cat', echoes Meg's secretive evening forays:

> *With a quiet, knowing stare,*
> *As the twilight grew darker,*
> *And night filled the air.*
> *With a purr and a stretch,*
> *He leaped onto the ledge,*

SPRING

And gazed at the moon's pale glimmer,
The light on the garden's edge.

On summer evenings, when I was made to go to bed before deep dusk, she would keep me company as the light faded. There, she'd play with aggressive good humour, hugging my wriggling foot with her front paws while walloping it with her hind legs, and chewing it into submission. Spring, however, was always the time when twilight caterwauling would begin. I grew up in a liminal zone of my own – a no-man's land between suburb and agricultural land – where pampered felines rubbed shoulders with farm cats under the cover of dusk. When the days began to lengthen, as we slipped out of winter, unneutered moggies would sing at the top of their voices from dry stone walls and dustbins.

Domesticated cats are different from their wild cousins in two key ways. Unlike dogs, which are a pack animal, wild cats are a solitary species by nature. Domestication has meant they have had to adapt to tolerate not only humans but also the company of other cats. Apart from that, however, the behaviour and anatomy of the domestic cat (*Felis catus*) is remarkably similar to its wild counterpart – the wild cat (*Felis silvestris*). And, although humans 'keep' cats as pets, and feed them generously, the cat has never lost its instinct to hunt. Twilight is prime killing time. The domestic cat is perfectly designed to stalk the garden at low light, when much of its prey is active. While humans have excellent colour vision and have superior distance vision to cats, our feline friends excel at seeing in dim light, detecting motion, and have a wider field of view. Cats' eyes also possess a *tapetum lucidum*, a reflective surface that causes their eyes to appear as if they glow in the dark. It's a true superpower and one that many animals who live in the half-light possess. Essentially a tiny mirror at the back of the eye, it bounces light back through the retina, giving the eye a second chance to capture it. What cats can't do, however, is see in complete darkness. Cats have also evolved sleeping patterns that allow them to peak at twilight. Throughout any given 24-hour period, a cat will snooze for an average of between 13 and 17 hours a day. This extended period of rest allows cats to preserve enough energy to do frantic but focused hunting under the cover of low light. Even kittens, and senior cats who have lost much of their predatory urges, still follow this crepuscular routine, channelling it into bursts of play, vocalisations and half-light wanderings.

I've also noticed that my eyesight plays tricks in the low light of a twilit garden. Red petals look weirdly dark in dimness, in a way that just doesn't happen with other colours, while purply blue flowers, especially the clematis, almost glow. Turns out it's not just my imagination. It's called the Purkinje effect and is particularly noticeable with geraniums. In the middle of the day, their showy flowers are a bright, pillar-box red against deep, dark green leaves. At half-light, the contrast switches and it is the flowers that appear dark and the leaves oddly bright. It's an optical quirk that was first spotted by Czech physiologist Jan Evangelista Purkinje in the early 1800s. As a medical student, Purkinje would take long, rambling walks in the countryside where he noticed that, after sunset, the colours in the meadows and margins seemed to change. Red blossoms and petals appeared darker while blue flowers remained bright. Science has since revealed that, in low illumination, our eyes can detect blue flowers better than any other colour, while red blooms and green leaves quickly appear to blacken in the half-light.

The gardener poet, Vita Sackville-West, spent hours in her garden, around dusk, and loved how the dying light altered the mood and look of her planting. Of phlox, she wrote, 'It does give a sumptuous glowing show, especially if you can plant it in a half-shady bed where its colours will curiously change with the sinking sun and will deepen with twilight into colours you never thought it possessed.'[16] She also loved how twilight gave pale flowers an uncanny hue: 'There comes a moment of twilight when white plants gleam with a peculiar pallor or ghostliness [...] The ice-green shades that it can take on in certain lights, by twilight [...] make a dream of the garden, an unreal vision, yet one knows that it isn't unreal at all because one has planted it all for effect.'[17] Ghostly petals, glow-worms and intoxicating perfumes; the garden at twilight is truly an enchanted place.

3

Dusk Perfume, Dead Flesh Flowers and Picky Sheep

To say John Gerard had green fingers is a chronic understatement. Although he initially trained as a barber-surgeon, a grisly career that encompassed both trimming hair and brisk amputation, he found he was also rather good at the quieter art of horticulture. While studying in London, he began creating a garden in Holborn, filling it with seeds and plants from around the world. By 1597 he had collected and successfully grown hundreds of species, many very rare. He had also learned enough to write and publish his now celebrated *Herball, or Generall Historie of Plantes*, a mighty volume containing more than a thousand plants and their uses.

In it, he described one particular species as 'The Marvel of Peru' but suggested perhaps the name 'Marvel of the World' might be more apposite. For this remarkable plant was not only enchantingly exotic, a Spanish treasure recently plundered from South America, but it also exhibited some rather unusual behaviour. Unlike most of the plants familiar to Gerard, which bloomed during the day, the 'Marvel of Peru' did the opposite. Its flowers opened as the Sun set. From then until dawn, it would emit a heady, intoxicatingly sweet perfume 'and so continue until eight of the clock the next morning'.[1]

The marvel of Peru, once only found in tropical areas of the American continent, is now a common all-garden plant across the world. Its flowers do indeed open at dusk, giving rise to two of its better-known English folk names – the four o'clock flower or pretty-by-night. Indeed, many countries have named the plant after its astonishing habits – in France it is the *belle de nuit*, in Norway the *mirakelblom*. In Turkey it is the *aksam sefasi*, evening pleasure, in Russian the *nochnaya krasavitsa* or night beauty. And, while John Gerard was clearly struck by the eccentric flowering of the marvel of Peru, it turns out there are plenty of plants that are crepuscular and do amazing things at twilight. A quick amble around any cottage garden, straight after sunset, will reveal a surprisingly broad selection of plants beginning their evening seduction. Certain species of lily, honeysuckle, campions, petunias, night-scented stock, pinks (dianthus), angel's trumpet, mock orange, sweet rocket, tobacco plant, night phlox, wisteria, jasmine, and evening primrose, to name but a few, all start to release their fragrance as daylight levels fall. Some wildflowers are also sweet-scented at twilight, including the night-flowering catchfly, bladder campion, and musk mallow.

Plants and pollinators have evolved a mutually beneficial arrangement. Like any good marriage, there is plenty of give and take. Plants need pollinators to maximise their chances of reproductive success and pollinators rely on flowers for food. And, while we might imagine that most pollination is performed by the assiduous efforts of day-flying honeybees and butterflies, an equally important but largely ignored group of pollinators starts its shift as the Sun goes down. Moths and bats are perhaps the best known of these half-light superheroes but a surprising number of other pollinating creatures come out when the Sun dips below the horizon. Across the world, these include certain species of ants, flies, beetles, rodents, cockroaches, thrips, reptiles, birds and mammals. Emerging under the cover of twilight, these evening-shift pollinators can forage in relative safety, away from daytime predators or hot weather, and avoid having to compete for delicious, energy-rich nectar with other wildlife.

Twilight pollination, however, comes with its challenges, not least the fact that light levels are low and many creatures struggle to see in the gloom. And so, many crepuscular plants have developed remarkable strategies for enticing their favourite guests to visit after sunset, including possessing bewitching, irresistible fragrances. Scientists have studied theses dusk scents and found that plants pollinating either at dusk or dawn often have unusually strong scent profiles.[2] Different species of flowers who share little in common apart from the fact that they are pollinated by species of hawkmoths, for example, all release intense, clove or incense-like fragrances.[3]

In fact, most of the world's highly aromatic flowers are crepuscular. The night-flowering jasmine, for instance, is reputed to be the planet's most potently fragranced bloom. Nineteenth-century poets loved the plant's slightly risqué connotations – a flower that only truly revealed its secrets when the lights went down. Thomas Moore, whose erotic poetry titillated London's high society, penned an ode typical of the times: 'From timid jasmine buds, that keep / Their odour to themselves all day, / But, when the sunlight dies away, / Let the delicious secret out / To every breeze that roams about', but there are plenty more, just as beautifully fragrant examples dotted throughout the century.

By contrast, a number of crepuscular plants are absolute stinkers. The fabulously named midnight horror tree, native to the Indian subcontinent, has twilight-opening flowers that smell truly appalling to humans but are absolute catnip to pollinating bats. And the stomach-turning Indonesian corpse flower, which only blooms every few years, begins to release its sickeningly fetid perfume between mid-afternoon and late evening to attract crepuscular carrion beetles and flesh flies. Such is the drama of a corpse flower 'reveal' that prize specimens in national collections have become tourist attractions in their own right. 'Putricia', a corpse flower in the Royal Botanic Gardens of Sydney, bloomed in January 2025 for the first time in fifteen years. Such was the media buzz that 8,000 people watched it unfurl online and thousands more visited Putricia in person to experience a smell uniquely described as 'wet socks, hot cat food, or rotting possum flesh'.[4] Only six months earlier, in London's Kew Gardens, a BBC science journalist had described its corpse flower's stench as 'a whiff of unwashed lavatory with strong undertones of something that went off at the back of the fridge'.

Even Britain's polite gardens aren't immune to twilight stenches. The stinkhorn fungus is common in the UK, and most of mainland Europe, and is as at home in a suburban back garden as it is in its native habitat of deciduous woodland. It also absolutely reeks. Many people, when they first smell it, mistake it for blocked drains, but its whiff – which closely resembles decomposing flesh – is designed to attract crepuscular blowflies, which will inadvertently carry the fungus's spores away with them. Its Latin name – *Phallus impudicus*, 'shameless penis' – comes from its alarming resemblance and rapid, turgid emergence from the forest floor. At dusk, in autumn, it starts to tumesce, like something from a seaside postcard. What begins looking like a badly wrapped hen's egg suddenly bursts open and its stalk thrusts upwards, growing to around six inches in height in just a few hours. Come dawn, it'll start to wither and die, but not before its cadaverous scent has wafted far and wide. Stinkhorn's other name was wood witch, a moniker derived from its malevolent pong, and the only way to tackle it was, in folklore, to burn it. Even Charles Darwin's daughter, Henrietta, hated the poor old *Phallus impudicus*. She famously dug up all the stinkhorns in her garden at Down House 'and burnt [them] in the deepest secrecy on the drawing-room fire'.[5]

Floral fragrances are a potent mix of volatile chemicals. In many plants, these compounds are released at certain times dictated by their circadian clocks. In petunias, for instance, evening twilight tells the plant to release a mix of benzaldehyde, a fruity, almondy odour, and vanilla-like phenylpropanoids, creating a rich, wonderfully intense smell.[6] In the daytime, however, petunias emit very little scent at all. The release of these perfumes has been shown to be controlled by specific proteins, which in turn respond to changes in light colour picked up by the plant's photoreceptors.

It's an amazing process and much of it is still a mystery: scientists still don't know, for example, why some dusk-scented flowers only emit fragrance if they have their roots in the soil. In an almost fable-like lesson, anyone who cuts a hoya flower in the hope of stealing its dusk scent will find the severed bloom stubbornly refuses to release its perfume. Other studies have indicated the dusk-flowering blooms seem to adjust the potency of their perfumes depending on how much nectar is left or how long the flower has been blooming, as if to signal to pollinators whether to bother visiting at all.

What is clear, however, is that a strong perfume travels particularly well in the dusk-to-dawn window. The character of the weather from sunset to sunrise is very different from the daytime. As a general rule, temperatures are lower at dusk (and their chilliest just before dawn). This end-of-day cooling reduces the likelihood of severe storms and decreases wind turbulence; the amount of water vapour in the air also increases.[7] With fewer erratic gusts and higher humidity, odour molecules released by dusk blooms remain in the air for longer, and carry further. This is a boon for insects, such as moths, that have a superb sense of smell and can detect odours at distances well over a kilometre. Writers have noticed this evening stillness and wrote about it with a familiarity that has perhaps now been lost. In *Anne of Green Gables*, first published just after the turn of the nineteenth century, its author Lucy Maud Montgomery wrote with the easy confidence of someone who had experienced twilight after perfumed twilight:

> The light was softening into twilight, and the air was filled with that sweet, delicate fragrance of evening which seems to come from the very earth itself. The sky was a pale, silvery blue, with a few faint, rosy clouds lingering in the west. Overhead the first stars were beginning to shine, and the moon was rising slowly, a great, round, golden disk. Everything was hushed and still. Even the wind seemed to hold its breath, as if it, too, were pausing to gaze upon the beauty of the twilight hour.

A heady fragrance is just one mechanism for attracting pollinators at twilight. In the half-light, many insects have vision capable of exploiting even the slightest glimmer of light. The Central American sweat bee, for example, buzzes from flower to flower in thick rainforest for only two short periods in the day – about an hour after sunset and another hour before dawn. Light levels in the dark canopy are very low at these times, but the sweat bee can weave and flit among the leaves because it has evolved eyes that are thirty times more sensitive than its day-flying bee cousins.

Other insects seem to have the ability to detect colour in almost complete darkness. While we humans struggle to see colour in low light, it has already been shown that hawkmoths, bull ants, carpenter ants and some species of bee have very light-sensitive eyes and can detect colour even in the dingiest of twilights. By becoming extremely sensitive to even the most minute amount of light, some of these crepuscular creatures have probably reduced their ability to see fine detail or detect movement, but other senses – such as smell – seem to help them fill out the picture.

Twilight can be a chilly time for a flying insect and so some crepuscular pollinators, such as moths, have evolved a covering of fine hairs. Being plump and fluffy gives moths a thermodynamic advantage, keeping them cosy on cool evenings so they don't have to expend too much energy keeping warm. A number of crepuscular plants, such as Mexican magnolias, seem to 'know' that twilight insects need warming up and offer heat as a way of enticing them to stop by. Their flower heads act as small heat collectors or 'solar furnaces' with temperatures inside their compact blooms invitingly warmer than the ambient evening air.[8] The hawkbit, a dandelion-like wildflower, closes up shop for the night more often than not with a pollen beetle snugly tucked inside. Come the morning, the petals reopen and the rested beetle can be on its way.

Perhaps the canniest of all crepuscular flowers, however, has to be the giant water lily. A native of South America, it pulls out all the stops – fragrance, visual appeal and warmth – to attract the scarab beetle. The giant lily is a botanical garden crowd pleaser, with its huge floating lily pads big enough to keep a toddler afloat. Come sunset, its buds open to reveal a huge dinner tray of a flower, nearly half a metre across. The flower then begins to exude an intoxicating, butterscotch-pineapple perfume. Any scarab beetle tempted to crawl inside the flower to find the nectar will also discover its surroundings are a balmy 12°C warmer than outside. The plant wants the beetle to linger and so, when dawn arrives, it will close up its petals and trap the insect inside. The beetle will remain captive, gorging on nectar and getting cloaked in pollen, until the following dusk when the lily will reopen and let its prisoner go free.

The world of crepuscular pollination is one which science is only just beginning to understand. It's also proving to be more richly populated, and much more ecologically important to humans, than we ever imagined. While some plants can only be pollinated by one specific pollinator – the yucca plant and crepuscular yucca moth, for example, are bound in an unshakeably exclusive pact – other plants hedge their bets and try to attract daytime, crepuscular and nocturnal pollinators. In a study that monitored an English meadow over repeated 24-hour periods, for example, it was shown that there was never any hour, in the entire day/night rotation, that insects weren't out and about pollinating. Flies, bees and wasps were the most abundant visitors during the day, while moths and beetles took over from dusk until dawn. Furthermore, of the seven most visited meadow flowers, five species were promiscuous and pollinated by both day- and evening-shift insects.[9]

Commercial crops also benefit from twilight visitors. Bats, for example, pollinate the particular species of agave that produces tequila. Crepuscular beetles fertilise nutmeg. Thrips, perhaps better known as thunder flies, play a big role in pollinating aubergines, palm oil, elderflower and coffee at dusk.[10] Some plants like avocado can even switch between day and dusk flowering, depending on climatic conditions, in the hope that some creature will visit.[11] And, while most of the literature and evidence comes from tropical regions, the work performed by these out-of-hours pollinators even shapes our rural landscape closer to home. Crops such as radishes, peas and strawberries are all visited by crepuscular moths. One study of the English agricultural landscape and its pollinators showed that over a hundred moth species – from owlet moths to tiger moths – were fluttering around under the cover of dim light pollinating members of the rose, bean, carrot and mint families.[12] Other studies have shown that across different environments, from urban allotments to rural orchards, crepuscular moths were frequently pollinating plants that no-one thought they even bothered with. These included lime, sycamore and ash trees, and a delicious summer-pudding trio of redcurrants, blueberries and raspberries.[13] [14]

Pollinators aside, the relationship between plants and twilight is truly fascinating. Remember our Greek philosopher Theophrastus and his tamarind tree, from Chapter 2, the plant that closed its leaves at dusk and opened them at dawn? We now know that this ability is called 'nyctinasty'. Lots of plants exhibit nyctinastic behaviour, allowing their leaves to fold, droop or curl up at the end of the day. Some flowers, including poppies, celandines, crocuses, tulips and water lilies, do the same with their petals, closing them up tightly as twilight falls, only to reopen at first light. Others, such as lady's smock and wood anemone, droop their petals at dusk only to rise again at dawn.

Another morning twilight wildflower, goat's-beard, unfastens its straggly dandelion-like petals at dawn, only to close them tightly just before midday. Country folk not only knew the flower by its prompt crepuscular timing, calling it 'Jack-go-to-bed-at-noon', but boiled and ate its roots as valuable sustenance. Many people who relied on the fruits of countryside foraging would have had an intimate acquaintance with the operating hours and behaviour of rural plants and flowers, a common knowledge that is now largely lost. John Gerard, our fan of the Marvel of Peru, also knew the Jack-go-to-bed-at-noon, a flower that 'shutteth itself at twelve of the clock, and showeth not his face open until the next day', and heartily recommended its delicious roots 'buttered as parsnips and carrots'.[15] In fact, such was the interest in the chronological behaviour of flowers, both native and exotic, that seventeenth-century English poet Andrew Marvell imagined a clock made entirely of flowers that opened and closed at different hours of the day. In his poem, 'The Garden', he imagined this horticultural time-piece:

*How well the skillful gard'ner drew
Of flow'rs and herbs this dial new,
Where from above the milder sun
Does through a fragrant zodiac run;
And as it works, th' industrious bee
Computes its time as well as we.
How could such sweet and wholesome hours
Be reckon'd but with herbs and flow'rs!*[16]

From prayer plants, whose leaves turn upwards at dusk like beseeching hands, to the shameplant, whose foliage closes meekly at sunset, many nyctinastic plants can thank their crepuscular habits for their monikers. And yet, while botanists suspect the behaviour is triggered by changes in the intensity or spectral quality of light at twilight, no-one actually knows why plants exhibit this behaviour. Charles Darwin identified over a hundred plants - from garden lupins to wild sorrel - that had strange 'sleep movements' and thought it might be something to do with plants protecting themselves from night frosts. Darwin and his colleagues performed many experiments with nyctinastic plants, late into the evening. Leaves were pinned down to cork boards, like cartoon heroines on railway lines, unable to wrestle free as dusk wore on. Without being able to move under the cover of twilight, many of the leaves were shrivelled or dead by morning, a result that Darwin attributed to frost exposure. Many plants that twist, curl or go limp after sunset, however, grow in areas that never experience sub-zero temperatures, and so other suggestions for nyctinasty have been thrown into the ring. Newer research suggests that plants might close their petals or leaves as a way of keeping their pollen intact or disguising themselves from evening herbivores. The truth is, however, yet to unfurl.

Plants must also perform some remarkable twilight maths. During the day, plants busily photosynthesise, converting sunlight, carbon dioxide and water into sugar and oxygen. They use this sugary energy to feed their growth. At night, plants can't make any more sugars so they draw upon energy reserves they made the preceding day. But there's a problem with this. In many parts of the world, night lengths vary throughout the year. If a plant used up its stored sugars at the same rate every night, there would be plenty of occasions when it would run out of fuel and die before the next sunrise. And so, plants make an astonishing calculation at dusk. If the dusk to dawn window is going to be a long one, the plant will work out that it needs to carefully ration its sugar reserves. If it's summer and the night is set to be brief, it'll use up its reserves more quickly and put on more growth. If the plant gets its rationing correct, its sugars are exhausted just after morning's twilight has finished.

And, while this silent miracle of energy regulation goes largely unnoticed, livestock farmers and horse owners are only too aware of the difference in nutrition of late-afternoon grass, which is full of goodness, and morning grass, which is less nutritious. Studies with farm animals have shown that both sheep and cattle are expert at detecting these time-dependent sugar levels. Present a sheep with a pile of hay cut at dusk, and another cut at dawn, and it'll head for the evening fodder every time. Grazing animals often binge at dusk as most grasses, and legumes such as clover, will be at their most deliciously sweet and full of sugars at this late stage in the day, especially in spring and summer. One study of clover, for example, found it had almost three times as much sugar in the afternoon than in the morning.[17]

In fact, the world of agriculture is starting to become very interested in twilight indeed. Crops grow at different rates and flower at different times, depending on the time of year. For decades it was thought that only two factors influenced when a crop grew and flowered: temperature and day length. In other words, as spring slips into summer, plants respond to longer hours of sunlight and warmer weather. A recent study, however, found out that another factor might be controlling the process – twilight length. Biologists looked at mouse-ear cress, a relation of the cabbage and mustard family, and a plant closely studied over the years as a useful proxy for globally important crop species.[18] The researchers exposed mouse-ear cress to growing conditions with different simulated lengths of civil twilight – from zero to 90 minutes. Like Goldilocks's porridge, it turned out that mouse-eared cress grew larger, and with more flowers, when twilight was neither too brief nor too long – it responded best to a civil twilight of around an hour. While an interesting exercise in itself, there is a rather more compelling reason for pursuing the research. As climate change fuels hotter weather, severe droughts and more flooding, worldwide crops are taking a battering. Many foods – from cranberries to coffee, wheat to maize – are being farmed at more northerly latitudes to avoid the climate's extremes. Whether a crop will thrive in its new environment may not only depend on temperature, daylight hours and rainfall, but a complex interaction of factors including its twilights.

Twilight Diary

Spring/Summer

It's late April and about a quarter past four in the morning. Across the field, Andy, our cockerel, has started to crow. The gap in the curtains tells me it's still dark outside, but our trusted timekeeper is never wrong. It is about 90 minutes to sunrise. It's a blowy, sodden late spring morning but whatever the weather, or time of year, Andy runs like clockwork. When the cock-a-doodling begins, come rain or shine, I know morning twilight has begun its slow ascent.

It's an impressively loud crow up close. After a few initial gravelly throat-clearers, Andy gets into his stride. He raises his beak to the sky, lengthens his gloriously ruffled neck, and throws his head backwards, like an old-time crooner reaching their top note. When he's strutting about the farm, his crow is a cheerful head-turner. A volley of cock-a-doodle-doos in the confines of a small coop, however, must be deafening for the hens who share his roost. Soon, our other two bantam cockerels add their cries to the cacophony. Both younger and smaller than Andy, these two males never seem to crow quite as loudly, or with as much conviction, as the elder statesman. It's enough of a racket, however, to kill any chance of going back to sleep and my mind always begins to whir.

The Anglo-Saxons had an excellent word for dawn – *úht* – a lovely, pithy word that was often joined with others to denote specific morning twilight events. There's *úht-floga*, a creature that flies only at dawn; *úht-hlem*, a din made in the early hours of the morning; and *úht-sceaþa*, a twilight thief. My favourite phrase of all, however, is one that speaks of a thousand-year-old shared truth – *úht-cearu* or 'dawn cares' – those creeping, anxious thoughts that come when you're lying awake in the long minutes before sunrise.[1] Worries or not, however, the cockerels' rude awakening happens without fail. Every morning, throughout the year, regardless of the weather, they know to crow. They also know exactly when to crow. Before I kept chickens I always assumed that cockerels began to crow at sunrise, a simple response to the appearance of the Sun. And yet, this isn't what happens. Cockerels actually start their crowing well before sunrise, at some point during twilight.

On the farm, the evening's twilight also acts as a cue for all the chickens to head back home. When bird flu restrictions haven't got them in 'flockdown', our poultry are gleefully free range and roam surprisingly far from the coop during the course of the day. Just after sunset, they begin a casual saunter back to base. The changing light is a signal to have a final gorging on grain and then head inside the coop, to their designated spot on the roosting bars. It's a well-orchestrated affair and deeply hierarchical, with Andy's favourite hens enjoying closer proximity to him than the also-rans. Before too long, the coop falls into a companiable, collective slumber.

The runner ducks and Wanda, our embden goose, also follow twilight's cue and amble back to their hut. While not quite as well behaved and regimented as the hens, their behaviour noticeably changes in the half-light. Putting the ducks and goose to bed involves gently coaxing them up a ramp into their large hut. Attempt to do it before twilight and the fowl will simply refuse to go in, instead taxiing around the enclosure like aeroplanes waiting to land. Leave it too late, after darkness has arrived, and the gaggle have often fallen asleep outside on the grass. In twilight, however, their mood changes. They become strangely biddable. Catch them at dusk and a few simple words of encouragement are all it takes for the ducks and Wanda to make a beeline for bedtime. The line-up into the hut is always the same. Goose first, the blushing bride, followed by her quacking bridesmaids.

Late spring's lengthening days seem to rocket-charge all the ducks' sex drives. Male ducks are fairly aggressive lovers at the best of times but, at this period in the year, the red mist descends and they go into overdrive. The runner duck drakes – all named Steve because we can't tell them apart – start to roam further than normal in a desperate search for females. They make a beeline for the neighbouring farm and have one destination in mind – the disgusting, muddy drainage ditches that outline the fields. Wild ducks sometimes nest in these secret channels, and I suspect the Steves know this. They'll rush out at dawn and spend the daylight hours wandering up and down these deep trenches, hidden from view. Only when twilight falls will they abandon their fruitless search for romance and waddle home, their pristine white feathers blackened with sludge. I'm always amazed by their ability to pick their way home in the dying light – one grassy ditch looks very like another and they stretch for miles. I suspect the Steves rely on some other cue, along with eyesight, to find their way back to their hut. Dusk smells, perhaps, or something else invisible.

One species of duck we keep, however, resists being cooped up at twilight. All domestic ducks are derived from the mallard, apart from the muscovy, a large breed that stubbornly retains its untamed nature. At dusk, rather than head for indoor shelter, our muscovy duck Dolly will take to the skies and find a safe roosting place. On the farm, the top of a barn door or a high tree will do just nicely, a throwback no doubt to her ancestral forest beginnings and the need to find a safe place to snooze after sunset fell.

Although scientists are only just beginning to explore the relationship between twilight and farmed animals' circadian rhythms, there's no doubt that the kaleidoscopic shift in light intensity and colour that only happens at twilight is profoundly important for the poultry here on the smallholding. Animal researchers are also just discovering that the way we rear animals, such as chickens, on a commercial scale often fails to take into account the subtle circadian cues that are needed to keep a creature content. There's plenty of rather depressing research that's worked out how to get the greatest number of eggs, or fastest growth rate, from indoor-reared chickens by tweaking artificial light levels. Meat birds kept in constantly low light conditions, for example, tend to eat more and move around less (expending fewer calories), a double win for farmers hoping to super-size their flocks.

A more nuanced look at the effect of artificial lighting on poultry, however, has shown that allowing birds to have lighting that mimics the day's transition into night, and back again in the morning, makes for happier, healthier birds. As I have seen first-hand with my own flock, chickens use twilight cues for much of their natural behaviours – from knowing when to roost to eating a last meal before a long night. Hens also use morning twilight as a cue to start grooming themselves and searching for water. In commercial settings where lights flick instantly on and off, without simulated twilight, chickens are forced to do one of two things. Like an avian version of musical chairs, the birds either dangerously scramble for a roosting spot in the dark or, more likely, are left stranded on the floor, unsure of what to do next.

In late spring, every year, an extended family of house sparrows starts to make a racket in the gutters above our bedroom window. From then until August, a caravan of between ten and twenty of these small birds returns from the surrounding fields and woodland to nest in the eaves. They're fabulously social and, unlike many other garden birds, seem to enjoy each other's company. House sparrows build their nests in colonies, like a row of terraced houses, and prefer to live cheek-by-jowl. They cheerfully shout at each other, starting well before sunrise, a cacophony of tuneless chelp-churrups and tweets. It's so loud both my husband and I are often woken by their festival carousing and must doze with pillows over our heads. I rather like their incessant jabbering, but my husband, who works long, physical hours, begrudges their early start.

The house sparrow irked the Victorian ornithologist. One of the joys of modern conservation, and nature writing, is the sense that all nature should be valued; there are no 'good' and 'bad' creatures, each is an integral cog. No such egalitarianism worried the nineteenth-century naturalist, who freely aired his views about those species who failed to please. The house sparrow, it seems, was a thoroughly bad egg. Its early dawn, laddish behaviour was far too unruly for polite society. House sparrows were, in no uncertain terms, the oiks of the avian world. There are some wonderfully irate descriptions of the house sparrow in old birding books; 'its yelping concerts', one volume complains, 'are an intolerable nuisance, and for this offence alone, I should, without the smallest objection, see the bird exterminated from the land...'. Remarkable words from a nature writer.

There was also something about society, and the underclass, that Victorian writers saw in the bird's out-of-hours habits. Words such as 'rude', 'mischievous' and 'thieving' were often employed in descriptions of this chatty, convivial bird. Gentleman ornithologist Neville Wood, who published his *British Song Birds* at the precociously tender age of eighteen while living at Sudbury Hall in Derbyshire, even went so far as to call the house sparrow 'radically plebian' and worthy of the 'train of maledictions poured on its hapless head'. Sparrows were also charged with being libidinous, perhaps because they noisily raised three or four broods a year. 'He was as hot and lecherous as a sparrow,' wrote Chaucer in *The Canterbury Tales*, and he 'Kissed her sweetly, chirping like a sparrow'; Shakespeare, too, repeats the same belief in *Measure for Measure*: 'Sparrows must not build in his house-eaves because they are lecherous'. So many human failings to foist upon one bird.

One of the sparrow's perceived faults was that, although it sang at dawn, its voice wasn't considered a patch on other members of the dawn chorus. There are plenty of other spring songbirds on the farm, ready to pipe up at morning's twilight. The earliest to start are often the robins in the orchard, whose rippling, animated whistling can be heard all year round and as early as nautical twilight. Soon after, the song thrushes in the beech hedge join the churring medley. The fluty, effortless blackbird also begins, the loveliest of all dawn carollers, followed by a mixed melody of chiffchaffs, goldfinches and the gentle 'who-who-who-who-whoooo' of the wood pigeon. The wren too – a bird with a giant voice for such a tiny frame. It's a glorious, spirit-lifting symphony but surprisingly brief. About half an hour after sunrise, almost every bird is out of puff and the tunes slowly filter away in the warmth of the morning. Our fascination with the dawn chorus is timeless. And yet, the more we learn, the less it seems to be about a glorious and cheerful symphony of bird song. Think bad-tempered shouting match rather than soothing melody. More pub brawl than avian choristers.

For all its charms, the dawn chorus is still a bit of a mystery. There's been plenty of research into why birds sing between nautical twilight and sunrise and the subject keeps on teasing out new and interesting threads. The first gramophone recording of bird song – a nightingale – wasn't released in England until 1910 and, since that time, scientists have captured and listened to endless twitterings in the hope of decoding their meanings.

Most ornithologists agree that the dawn chorus is predominantly performed by males and seems to serve two main purposes: mate attraction and territory defence. Within these two broad categories, however, there are lots of lovely nuances – birds will produce slightly different songs or sing to different audiences depending on what they are trying to communicate. For example, a bird might trill one song to attract a mate, but another slightly tweaked version to keep the same partner interested after mating. Other songs seem to be about sharing information with a friendly neighbour or warning off a potential rival. New studies also suggest that the dawn chorus might be performed to deter predators and that female birds often join the cacophony, albeit more quietly. One study even showed that the female dove's gentle cooing at dawn stimulates its own body to start ovulating in preparation for daytime mating.[2]

And why dawn in particular? Why not straight after sunrise or, even, all day long? This too isn't fully resolved. While many birds will carry on singing in short spurts during the day, the general consensus is that the songs warbled at dawn are more elaborate and louder than those sung at other times. One theory is that, rather like collective amnesia, during the night birds of the same species forget whose patch belongs to whom and what the pecking order is. Dawn is therefore the first moment in a new day when hierarchies and territorial borders can be noisily reaffirmed. Another idea is that female birds are at their most fertile at dawn and so male birds must put on their best vocal recitals first thing. Singing when light levels and temperature are both low, as is the case at morning's twilight, may also be a good use of a bird's time, one that doesn't eat into its daytime schedule of foraging. Singing under the cover of half-light also lowers the chances of drawing the attention of predators. The sound of bird song too benefits from optimal sound transmission at dawn – it is not only a quiet time compared to the hustle and bustle of daytime but, as we already know, atmospheric conditions allow songs to carry further.

Each performer, singing their heart out, is trying to demonstrate what a catch they are. A bird's ability to belt out physically demanding and complex songs can reflect its overall health and genetic strength – the more impressive and loud the voice, the more alluring a female will find the tenor. One interesting piece of recent research even suggests that the quality of a bird's performance actually improves as dawn slides into sunrise. A study of sparrows, for example, showed that – over the duration of any one morning session – the complexity and number of songs gradually improved as dawn progressed. The sparrows seem to 'warm up', like any singing professional, and smash out their best performance at the finale.[3]

Researchers have also found some interesting links between the biology of different bird species and their position in the dawn roll call. Birds that sing very early, often beginning at nautical twilight, have large eyes relative to their body size. They also tend to eat earthworms, rather than rely solely on daytime flying insects or grain. And so, this might explain why it is the robin, blackbird and thrush who pipe up first in the morning. All three of these birds are dedicated earthworm eaters, a creature that comes to the surface to mate and find food during the twilight. With their enhanced vision in low light, these avian early-risers steal the lead. Waking up early allows these performers to get their dawn chorus out of the way and begin foraging for breakfast while many other birds are still snoozing. The early bird really does catch the worm.

At the end of the day, at dusk twilight, there is often a second performance – usually from the robin, blackbird and goldfinch. There are fewer musicians at this hour but it's perhaps even more lovely than its dawn equivalent. Why some birds sing again at evening twilight isn't certain but it may be a chance for males to reaffirm their territories, those first established in the morning, in the still air and half-lit safety of dusk. I also hear different birds at evening's twilight, those perhaps drowned out at dawn's crescendo – the blue tit, the tree sparrow and dunnock – and often strain to work out exactly who is singing in the dimness. It's an altogether more subdued performance than the vigorous dawn chorus and perfectly serene. And one that lets me know it's time to start thinking about winding down towards bedtime.

SPRING/SUMMER

*

In early summer, last year, another bird made itself known at dusk. Every evening, for a period of about two months, a male barn owl appeared from nowhere. My youngest daughter and I would watch out for it, obsessively. When it arrived, around half past eight without fail, we would rush out into the garden and watch it follow the same rigorous routine. Evening after evening, unless the rain kept it from flying, the barn owl would take a sweeping clockwise tour of the hay fields which, at that time of the year, were tall enough to hide plenty of squeaking rodents. The barn owl's flight seemed leisurely and thoughtful as it quartered back and forth, pausing only to hover over promising prey before banking away or dropping to the ground, talons splayed. Its endless swoops and lifts revealed the blindingly white underside of the barn owl's wings and chest, almost pink in the twilight glow, while the grass meadows blazed golden. All silently performed to the slowly diminishing backdrop of the dusk chorus.

A friend of mine who's an archaeologist and fellow smallholder, in a neighbouring valley, has a dilapidated cow shed that's also become a favourite haunt for local barn owls. She and I compare barn owl notes, like children playing Top Trumps. Every spring for the past few years, the same pair have returned to her byre and raised a small family in a shallow depression on the top of a stone wall. The chicks huddle together in the gloom, hissing at any unfamiliar noise. They sit and wait, wide awake in the twilight, for their parents to bring home a never-ending supply of scampering rodents and frogs caught en route to their spawning ponds. Watching the barn owl pair silently foray back and forth is one of life's unadulterated pleasures.

The sublime, soundless gliding of barn owls is made possible by their special feathers, which are velvet-soft and have tiny, combed fringes that dampen the noise created by turbulence. As with all superpowers, however, they have a weak spot, and the barn owl's kryptonite is rain. Fluffy feathers soak up water like a sponge, making it near impossible to fly, and so barn owls must hunt when the weather's set fair. Barn owls are usually crepuscular but if the weather has been consistently wet for weeks, you'll see them risking a hunting expedition in broad daylight.

I've seen these hungry owls out and about, over the years, especially in the afternoon. Back in

February, as I came down the farm track in my old Land Rover an hour before dusk, I noticed a thin barn owl perched on a fence post. They usually take flight if you approach but this one was rooted to the spot, concentrating on the scruffy grass verge below. The barn owl was so transfixed, it barely registered as I pulled up right next to it and turned off the engine; I must have been less than two metres away. The barn owl, famished from weeks of drizzle, stood for at least five minutes staring at the ground. Its bleached tail feathers were being buffeted by the cross wind that often whistles through the farm, and occasionally threatened to topple it over, but the barn owl remained determinedly fixed. It then dropped, almost clumsily, to the ground, wings outstretched. What I thought was, at first, a badly executed landing turned out to be the barn owl 'mantling' its prey; a behaviour where barn owls will shield their catch with their wings, to prevent other predators from stealing it. The grey, interminable weeks of rain had not only pushed the barn owl out, blinking, into the bright daylight, but, like a Victorian street urchin, forced it to greedily cover its bounty. Nothing, not even a stranger in a car, was going to stop it from its first decent catch in weeks.

Over the years on the smallholding, I've noticed how susceptible barn owls are to anything that threatens their short, crepuscular window for hunting. Weeks of wet spring weather can be devastating, but so can hard winters. The winter of 2009–10, when the farm was cut off for weeks in deep snow, was lethal for these ethereal birds. I remember the cold snap well – we were stranded for an anxious fortnight, unable to clear drifts from the steep farm track to the main road. Our old farmhouse had both open fires blazing away and still the window panes froze on the inside, as the outside thermometer stuck at -16°C and icicles as long as furled umbrellas hung from the corrugated barn roofs. In the Dutch barn, where we store the hay, we found two dead barn owls. Stiff as cardboard and horribly thin, they had clearly starved. All the small dusk-dwelling rodents that would have normally kept them satiated – the voles, mice and shrews – were carpeted under thick, impenetrable snow. I wondered whether the owl pair had snuck into the Dutch barn under the cover of twilight, in the hope of finding mice among the straw, and perhaps sought shelter atop one of the vast bales. In the past, farmers actively encouraged barn owls into their granaries after sunset, to keep rodents at bay over autumn and winter. Our barn held no such quarry for the hungry owls. I felt terrible that we'd made such poor hosts and resolved to do better. One wobbly ladder and an owl box later, I'd at least provided a warm home if it was wanted. The weather at twilight, however, was out of my hands.

4

Cock Crow and Sparrow's Fart

There is a scene in Shakespeare's *Romeo and Juliet* when our two lovers must part with the coming sunrise. They both hear bird song. Juliet hopes it is the nightingale, a sign that dawn is still hours away, but Romeo knows the truth: 'It was the lark, the herald of the morn,' he corrects her, sadly, 'I must be gone and live, or stay and die.'

It's a fabulously misty-eyed moment in the play, but perhaps one of the most interesting things about the scene is that Shakespeare employed birds, and their calls, to signal what time of the day it was. Theatregoers, even those who lived in the middle of a squalid, rapidly urbanising London, would have got the avian references. Medieval audiences would have known which birds sang in the evening, and those that trilled at dawn. Nightingales, as their name suggests, entertained our ears under the cover of darkness. The lark, by contrast, announced the arrival of morning twilight, those precious moments before the Sun rises.

Indeed, throughout history, we have listened out for the calls of different birds to tell us what time it is. As early as Roman times, the value of the crowing cockerel was already well understood. Pliny the Elder, writing in the first century, praised the cockerel for his alarm-clock tendencies:

> our Roman night-watchmen, a breed designed by nature for the purpose of awakening mortals for their labours [...] They are skilled astronomers, and [...] recall us to our business and our labour and do not allow the sunrise to creep upon us unawares[1]

In medieval times, 'cock crow' was particularly important. In monastic life, evening prayers were divided into four periods of devotion – sunset, midnight, cock crow and dawn. Of these, morning twilight's cock crow was the most important – not only did it signal the gentle beginning of a new day, but it also embodied one of the fundamental ideas of religious faith. That, through prayer, the faithful could banish darkness and welcome in spiritual light. In Wales, there is still a service called *Plygain* held in chapels around Christmas time. Thought to derive from the Latin for 'cock crow' – *pulli canto* – it was traditionally a service held between three and six in the morning, the hours of winter twilight.

For everyday folk, however, the cockerel's first holler was also a time to breathe a sigh of relief. The night held untold dangers, not least the fear that restless spirits were abroad. Only the call of the cockerel, in the early crepuscular hours, would dispel nocturnal fairies and demons. Shakespeare's Hamlet talked of the ghost who 'faded on the crowing of the cock', but the idea was old hat even in the early 1600s. Prudentius, a Roman Christian poet writing over a thousand years earlier, in the fourth century, had already conjured up ghosts that roamed 'beneath the dark's vast dome; But, when the cock crows, take their flight, Sudden dispersed in sore affright'.[2]

While 'cock crow' has a dignified ring to it, Northern English folk have no such airs and graces. For us, the beginning of twilight is 'sparrow's fart', the time of the morning just a few hours before daylight. The earliest written record of this brilliantly descriptive phrase is 1828; etymologist William Carr reluctantly added the 'truly ludicrous expression' to his earnest collection of Yorkshire-isms – *The Dialect of Craven*.[3] His stiff-collared sensibilities forced him to suggest the phrase might come from some 'Anglo-Saxon' confection – *sparkle-fert* – a phrase that almost certainly never passed the lips of any speaker of Old English. In reality, the phrase does what it says on the tin – the time of day so quiet you could hear the parps of a small bird.

The fact that cockerels crow in the early hours of the morning has been celebrated for as long as humans and chickens have lived side by side. And yet, even though this relationship is perhaps as old as twelve thousand years, we're only just starting to understand why cockerels crow. Researchers at Nagoya University in Japan put two choirs of cockerels through their paces. The first group were given access to 12 hours of daylight and 12 hours of night-time conditions, for a period of two weeks. The second group, by contrast, sat glumly in the dark for the full fortnight. As predicted, the first group of cockerels began crowing two hours before the onset of daylight – just like Andy. Interestingly, the cockerels who remained in virtual darkness for what must have felt like two interminable weeks also piped up at the correct time, even though they had no visual clues to whether it was dawn or dusk. Their circadian rhythms, as we already know, were desperately trying to keep time even in the absence of any clues about whether it was day or night.

It also seems that cockerels' twilight crowing serves a number of purposes. Observations of the domesticated chicken's closest wild relative, the red junglefowl of south-east Asia, indicate that early morning crowing is designed to reinforce a cockerel's position within his group. In the wild, junglefowl often live in loose groups of both males and females, and cockerels must assert their claims on their territories and hens. And the dominant cockerel does the most calling. Crowing in the wild tends to be limited to their short breeding season and begins around 1½ to 2 hours before sunrise, with very little cock-a-doodling during the day or the rest of the year. Domesticated chickens, by contrast, have been selectively bred to be fertile and lay eggs throughout the year. Uncoupled from any kind of seasonal fertility, a domestic cockerel will feel the urge to welcome the dawn, and announce his presence, every single day.

Twilight is also absolutely critical for wild birds, especially when it comes to migration. In fact, such is the unshakeable bond between the avian world and dusk, in particular, that many species of wild birds in captivity will attempt to spring their cages at certain times of the year and take part in a mass exodus.

Few nineteenth-century parlours were complete without a songbird, for example, miserably confined to a gilded cage. Trapped for the amusement of their owners, these birds were rarely allowed to exhibit any of their natural behaviours. While most people failed to notice the irritation of their incarcerated pets, a handful of writers did note that – for a few days every spring and autumn – their expensive prisoners would become particularly agitated. At dusk, their birds seemed to flutter with frustration, hop up and down on their perches, or even launch themselves skywards only to repeatedly smash against the bars. Ornithologist Robert Sweet watched with a studious lack of empathy as his own caged birds, various members of the warbler family, were driven to distraction by their urge to migrate back home:

> It is very curious to see them when in that state, their restlessness seems to come on them all at once, and generally in the evening; when they are sitting, seemingly, quite composed, they start up suddenly, and flutter their wings; sometimes flying direct to the top of the cage, or aviary; at other times, running backwards and forwards on their perches, continually flapping their wings, and looking upwards all the time [...] their agitation generally lasts on them about a fortnight, sometimes more and sometimes less; in the spring it seems strongest on them; at that season, they will sometimes flutter about the whole of the night.[4]

Some game birds also showed this same restless spirit. Quails, a favourite quarry among the shooting fraternity, are migratory and in winter will try to head as far south as Africa before returning to Britain in spring, to breed. Come the autumn, as one Victorian writer noted, quails kept in cages 'become very restless, and fluttered about their cages, as if they felt it was time for them to depart'. Around sunset and the beginning of evening twilight 'they began to struggle to get free, and continued all night uneasy. In the morning, the birds looked sad and disappointed.'[5]

Migration is a remarkable phenomenon. Many bird species take a twice-yearly long-haul flight, and travel between places that offer seasonal bounties of food and clement weather. These long-distance flights are taken in spring and autumn and often carried out under the cover of darkness. Why any bird, who is normally active during the day, would choose to disrupt its normal routine and fly in dim light isn't well understood. Suggestions such as lack of predators, lower wind turbulence and celestial navigation are all posited, but the truth is that we still don't know exactly why day-flying birds migrate between dusk and dawn or even how they do it.

One thing that is clear, however, is the importance of evening twilight to the timing of annual migrations. Many species of birds, when they feel the seasonal urge to migrate, begin a routine of pre-flight preparation. In the daytime this can involve eating copious amounts of food, the aim being to put on an extra 50 per cent of their body weight, mainly as fat, to fuel the journey. Some birds, to accommodate this extra load but remain aloft, will start to shrink their internal organs. To enable the bar-tailed godwit, for example, to fly nearly 7,000 miles non-stop from Alaska to New Zealand, it has to reabsorb tissue from its liver, kidneys and digestive system. Old feathers are also shed, and new, sleek ones grow in their place. Birds, especially younger, less experienced ones also start to take practice flights at dusk. These are thought to be a vital opportunity to hone their flying skills and learn how to navigate before the departure date. In the final few days before leaving, birds will also start to congregate in excitable twilight clusters.

When the date to leave finally arrives, birds seem to know exactly when to set off, even if they are alone. In a study of nearly 400 migratory songbirds, from nine different species, almost all set off in the window of civil twilight.[6] Timing is everything: leave too early and you've missed valuable daytime foraging, leave too late and you won't be able to travel as far in the safety of darkness. Like an aircraft marshal, the appearance of twilight tells millions of migratory birds it's time for take-off.

This pre-flight preparation is characterised by a feeling of intense agitation; the urge to migrate is so deeply ingrained that caged birds, even those kept in the confines of a gloomy windowless room, will start preparing for travel at the same time as their wild brothers and sisters. Such is the innate desire to voyage that, after sunset, captive birds will shun slumber and begin a series of excitable, frustrated movements, as seen by Robert Sweet. They'll hop, whir their wings, and even launch off in the right direction as if heading to some well-known breeding or overwintering grounds. This innate restlessness has a name – *Zugunruhe* – a German word that combines *zug*, meaning to move or migrate, and *unruhe*, restlessness. In the wild this behaviour can last for anything between a day and a few weeks – the longer and more challenging the flight, the greater the duration of the *Zugunruhe*. And even though a caged bird has no chance of escape, come twilight it will experience the same urge to travel as its free cousins.

In autumn, vast congregations of starlings also take to the sky at dusk and form eerie shape-shifting waves. These are called murmurations and are one of nature's most mesmerising displays. The birds perform a synchronised aerial ballet; flocks splitting and merging, wheeling and banking, creating pulsing black clouds against the failing sky. While a feast for the eyes, there's a desperate tenacity to a murmuration. The starlings are fighting for their lives against one of dusk's most impressive aerial hunters – the peregrine falcon. It's the fastest bird on the planet and one who chooses civil twilight as its preferred killing time. The peregrine heads out as starlings begin to congregate in large groups to head for their evening roosting sites. Computer models of the patterns hidden within a murmuration reveal the starlings' attempts to baffle predators by flying in shapes that constantly flux in density and direction. At the approach of a peregrine, a murmuration will repeatedly expand, rupture and merge, creating amorphous, whirling masses that confuse the bird of prey and prevent it from isolating, and striking, any individual bird. If you're staring in wonder at an autumnal murmuration, pulsing in the twilight, there's a good chance a peregrine falcon also has it in its sights.

Twilight also belongs to the swift. This is a bird who spends almost its entire life aloft. It forages, mates and even sleeps 'on the wing', only ever landing to nest for a brief few weeks in any given year. At both dusk and dawn, the swift also performs a little-understood behaviour known as 'twilight ascents'. People had long noticed that, at dusk, swifts began to fly upwards, high towards the heavens, and it was long presumed they headed to these lofty elevations to seek calmer wind conditions that would allow them to sleep. More recently, science has revealed that swifts actually perform two twilight ascents – one at dusk and one at dawn. In summer, after sunset, swifts assemble in what are called 'screaming parties'. During civil and nautical twilight they perform their skyward ascent, reaching dizzying heights of up to two kilometres, before slowly dropping back down to Earth. Come dawn, they take the same journey again.

Research suggests that twilight - specifically the period between the beginning of civil twilight and the end of nautical twilight (when the Sun is between 0 and 12 degrees below the horizon) - offers swifts a chance to gather as much information as they can about distant weather patterns, their orientation, or local atmospheric conditions. In other words, swifts are using ascents to get their bearings. Twilight is the perfect time to do this; visual landmarks can still be seen in the dim light but stars and other celestial points are also visible. Swifts may also fly to high altitudes to access more settled weather and wind speed, both of which strongly affect the availability of the flying insects on which they rely.[7]

On the farm, we have a small copse of trees that we planted as a wedding present to ourselves. We asked guests to buy us, instead of plates or a trouser press, bundles of saplings. Beech, chestnut, cherry, ash, larch, birch - we heeled in as many deciduous species as we could get our hands on, and now, twenty years later, we have a small woodland where once there was a slurry pit and concrete pig barn. At dusk, in late spring, as the light begins to fail, it comes strangely alive with birds. Cock pheasants, which use our smallholding as a sanctuary from the local shoots, start to yell in the evening twilight – a sawing, shrill 'cok-cok, cok-cok'. They're calling out to females, and establishing their territorial boundaries, a last announcement into the blushing light before they flap noisily into the tree branches and perch for the night.

Once or twice, in the two decades we've been here, have I also heard the dusk calls of a woodcock. They're cunningly elusive and impossible to spot among the leaf litter and rotting bark. About the size of a huge jacket potato, with similar scorched brown colouring, the woodcock is an expert at camouflage and will lay low during the day. In late spring and early summer, however, the males will perform noisy and conspicuous twilight flights to attract a mate. These early evening displays – called 'roding' flights – are often mistaken for bats' erratic zigzagging and appear in silhouette against a gloaming sky. If you hear frog-like grunts and mice-like squeaking, however, it's almost certainly a male woodcock, calling out into the evening.

There is one bird possibly more adapted to crepuscular life than any other - the barn owl. Graceful, silent, deadly, it is a predator perfectly designed for this liminal time of the day. It hunts primarily by hearing, a sense that truly comes into its own under half-light. Dusk is a fantastic niche for any hunter that relies on its ears. It's beautifully peaceful, with diurnal creatures beginning their quiet rest phase. Moreover, the minute sounds of rustling voles and mice are more easily heard at twilight. Thanks to the peculiarities of sound waves, which travel differently depending on climate conditions, the cool temperatures and higher humidity experienced between dusk and dawn allow noises to travel further than in the daytime.

The barn owl's entire head is designed for listening: its large heart-shaped face acts like a satellite dish, picking up the smallest of scampers and squeaks. Many rodents are crepuscular and have peaks of frenzied activity just after sunset and just before dawn, no doubt to avoid nocturnal and daytime predators. Mice, under laboratory conditions, pick up speed and dash about with increasing mania as light levels approach those of sunrise, as if trying to run back to their burrows before sunlight exposes them to diurnal threats.[8]

Barn owls, however, have also embraced the crepuscular niche and, operating under the cover of dim light, they too avoid their own mortal enemies – the nocturnal tawny owl and day-flying buzzard and goshawks. In twilight the barn owl can hunt without fear or competition. And, while the barn owl's super sense is its hearing, its vision is also well adapted to crepuscular light. Its huge eyes have enlarged corneas and lenses, which capture even the feeblest scraps of light, while the same reflective layer that a cat possesses behind the retina – the *tapetum lucidum* – acts like a trampoline, bouncing light around inside the eye to improve its vision.

Perhaps the most remarkable of the barn owl's twilight adaptations is its plumage. For a bird that flies in dim light, it is curious that it has such conspicuously white feathers. Predators who sneak around in the shadows rarely advertise their presence. In fact, the whitest parts of the bird are its chest and under its wings, areas that are most visible to the barn owl's ground-level prey. What seems like a disadvantage, however, is actually one of the barn owl's most effective weapons. Barn owls use the glaring brilliance of their plumage to dazzle their prey. Rodents are very sensitive to light. When a mouse or vole sees flashes of light from above, it triggers a freeze response – like a deer in headlights. It seems barn owls use their snowy underwings and chest to reflect twilight's residual light or, if the Moon is out, its lunar glow.[9] Dazed and confused, rodents will stand motionless, unaware they're about to be snatched from above.

Another owl that flies around the farm is also crepuscular. Little owls are not strictly native, having been introduced from the Continent in the 1800s, but have become a feature of lowland countryside across England and parts of Wales. Sweetly diminutive, at no more than 20 centimetres high and weighing about the same as two hens' eggs, these mottled brown and cream birds have a less rigid routine than the barn owl and will often come out in the day. Their peaks of activity, however, are dusk and dawn. Twilight, at both ends of the day, is the time when the little owl's prey come out. Crepuscular insects – moths, crickets, beetles and earthworms – make up much of the little owl's catch, boosted with large helpings of rodents and small frogs, creatures who are also abroad in the half-light.

Yorkshire has the honour of being the first place little owls were most likely, if not entirely successfully, introduced. Gloriously eccentric landowner and naturalist, Charles Waterton, 'succeeded in bringing here, five of the little roman owls'[10] in the early 1840s, procured on one of his lengthy and often precarious adventures around Italy. On the Continent, little owls were often kept as pets or hunting lures for another twilight bird, the lark. At dawn, a little owl would be tethered as bait, the hunter knowing that a flock of larks would mob the poor owl, before swooping in with his net. Whatever happened to Waterton's little 'roman owls' isn't known, although he felt certain they had settled in nicely and become 'inhabitants of the woods'. It took decades, however, and subsequent introductions across the country for any sizeable population to take hold, not helped by the fact that fellow naturalists, when they did spy a little owl on home turf, promptly shot it and had it stuffed. Fellow of the Zoological Society, James Backhouse, cheerfully recalled just one incident of many, just 30 miles away from Waterton's estate, Walton Hall. In the 1897 edition of *The Naturalist*, he proudly recorded his brief brush with the 'very rare visitor':

> REALIZING to the full the meagre nature of the chronicles relating to the occurrence of the little owl (*athene noctua*) in Yorkshire, it is with no little satisfaction that I have to record the capture of a beautiful example near York. The specimen in question is an adult female, and was shot in the neighbourhood of Escrick, near York, on December 24th, 1896, being taken in the flesh to Mr. Edward Allen, of Feasgate, who has mounted it very ably.[11]

Here on the smallholding, the best time to see a little owl is at dawn, on an early summer's morning before sunrise. Then, they'll perch on a fence post, or the telegraph pole in the hill field, looking out for breakfast. Sometimes one will swoop down to the floor of the fold yard and bathe itself in the weak morning light. The crows, who often seem to work in pairs, quickly swoop in and chase it off, a dawn confrontation that the little owl has no hope of winning. Far from the farmyard, across the field, another, much more hidden, twilight battle rages silently at dusk and dawn. On the wild pond, winged crepuscular creatures swoop and dive near the water's surface. Others hover or stand near its margins, eyes fixed on the muddy shallows. And while a few are wild birds, like our friends from the dawn chorus, not every twilight visitor is who you'd expect...

Twilight Diary

Summer

It's June and the pond is churning with tadpoles. A few months back, dozens of frogs and toads slipped under the cover of half-light and made their pilgrimage here. Both species tend to return to the ponds of their birth, to meet, mate and lay their spawn, before heading back into the undergrowth. It's a remarkable and secret congregation.

I watch the pond with eagle eyes, looking for signs of life. Frogs and toads are sensibly shy – and often move under the cover of cool, damp twilight – so I rarely catch a glimpse of them in action. In fact, the only time I did get a sense of just how many frogs and toads visit our pond was as the result of a terrible mistake. The land around the water is dotted with trees. Rather than take a mower or strimmer to the woodland floor, both of which can be catastrophic for wildlife, my husband and I encourage our light-footed soay sheep to gently graze in between the trunks. To do this, we also need to erect a temporary electric fence – metres of flexible netting on poles that are unrolled and pushed into the ground.

Usually this happens at the end of summer, but one year we decided to let the sheep in early, during the first days of March. At dawn, the day after we had switched on the electric fence, I went down to see how the sheep were faring around the pond. To my utter horror, during the previous evening's dusk, dozens of frogs and toads – all of whom lived most of the year in the undergrowth or log piles around the farm – had attempted to reach their watery mating ground. Finding the netting in their way, many had tried to climb through it, only to be frazzled by the intermittent shocks an electric fence delivers. Every one of the thirty or so amphibians who had tried to run the dusk gauntlet had been electrocuted. Rather than fall off the netting the moment they expired, the frogs and toads were glued to the netting – like gruesome mannequins – as if posed mid-movement.

Some were even already paired up – small males clutching onto the back of larger females – and had died mid-amplexus embrace.

It was devastating to think that, in the attempt to be more sensitive to wildlife, we'd inadvertently caused harm. Needless to say, the electric fence came down immediately and we learned our lesson. Smallholding is not only about working with the seasons; nature is full of secret rituals and happenings, many of which we crash through like wrecking balls. Our solipsism blinds us to nature's complexity and routines – we barely know what happens beyond our limited experience. We had failed to realise that twilight was as busy on the farm as any other part of the day. It had also eluded us that ponds are important seasonal assembly places for populations who remain totally separate for most of the year – a sort of soggy Stonehenge.

We created the pond almost as soon as we arrived here. The farm sits in the bottom of a wide, shallow valley. It was once the bed of a large, post-glacial lake, and with enough early summer rainfall can start to feel that way again. Our sloping, pastured hillside is also called Spring Hill, a clue to the constant trickles that bubble under the soil. One field at the lowest point on the smallholding flooded regularly so we decided to go with the flow and create a large body of water that would work with the terrain and, more importantly, attract wildlife. It's been a roaring success without almost any intervention from us.

The pond itself has, almost magically, come to life. 'Spontaneous generation' – a once-held theory that life could spring from nothing – seems almost possible when a body of water starts to teem with wriggling, darting creatures. This life-from-nowhere was often believed to appear at deep twilight, a theory that would also explain why no-one saw it happening. The theory of spontaneous generation fooled even the brightest of scientific minds and held sway from the Greeks to the great age of Scientific Revolution in the seventeenth century. Looking at our pond, who could blame Aristotle for thinking that muddy slime created oysters or that fish sprang from the sand. Indeed, it was such a persuasive theory that folklore held on to some of its more outlandish claims well into the nineteenth century, including that notion that barnacles on ships turned into geese (which is why they're called barnacle geese) and that new honeybees emerged from rotting carcasses.

At the pond's muddy edges, I often find footprints; these are sometimes the only indication of the crepuscular creatures that come to drink.

Badgers, foxes, deer and hedgehogs all assemble at the watering hole under the safety of dusk and dawn. One of England's most iconic children's stories, *The Wind in the Willows* by Kenneth Grahame (1908), captured waterside twilights for generations of young readers like me:

> It was a beautiful evening, with a clear sky, the last rays of the sun turning the river into a stream of gold. The twilight deepened, and the first star twinkled faintly in the soft blue sky. The air was warm and sweet, and the river, still as glass, reflected the colours of the sky and the trees with a perfect clearness. The little creatures of the riverbank were busy preparing for the night, and the silence of the hour was filled only by the soft murmur of the water and the rustle of the leaves.

Another native waterside creature is also crepuscular, although few people know they have dawn and dusk lifestyles. Otters are half-light dwellers and twilight is their most productive hunting period for amphibians, fish and snoozing water-birds. The River Rye, which meanders close to our smallholding, has a well-established pair. Most of the time, they remain frustratingly elusive. They only seem to give themselves away occasionally, to early morning fishermen or dusk dog walkers, with a flash of their fat, shiny tails as they plunge under the thick flow.

The occasional deep dip into the depths of our pond, scooping into the black, rotted sludge that has slowly collected on its bed, reveals a cocktail party of glorious, uninvited guests. It is always thrilling to see great crested newts or fat, thumb-sized diving beetles. Pondlife folk names are also a delight and straight from the pages of a Victorian storybook – whirligig beetles, pond skaters, hoglouse, backswimmers and water boatmen. From the outside, the twilight pond is completely silent but there is a lively orchestra playing under its surface. Until recently, few people had really studied the soundscape of freshwater habitats and it turns out that, just like the birds have their dawn chorus, there is a bawdy twilight symphony played out by aquatic insects in ponds up and down the countryside. In a study led by ecologist Jack Greenhalgh, then at the University of Bristol's School of Biological Sciences, over eight hundred hours were dedicated to listening, using underwater microphones, to the creatures that lurked in ponds across southwest England. Two amazing things became almost instantly apparent:

the first was that, like the dawn chorus, there was a daily pattern to the freshwater fanfare. From dusk to dawn, pond life bursts into rhythm that continues through the night. Two peaks of musical activity also occurred during these late spring, early summer concerts – one between sunset and astronomical twilight and the other very early in the morning, between astronomical twilight and the beginning of civil twilight – roughly 8 p.m. to midnight and 2 a.m. until 4 a.m.

The second surprise to emerge from listening to pond song was that one species was far noisier than all the others. There are a number of freshwater insects that use their legs, like oars, to row across the water. Both the common backswimmer (which rows upside down, under the water) and water boatman (which scull on the surface) produce incredibly loud noises using the same technique as crickets or grasshoppers. Called stridulation, it involves rubbing two body parts together to make a sound, like a fingernail being dragged along a hair comb. For their tiny size, water boatmen and backswimmers make an impressive din and one species in particular trumps them all. At just two millimetres in length, the lesser water boatman is among the smallest of all the oarsmen but turns out to be a champion musician. On an average performance, he will easily reach 80 decibels, noisier than a vacuum cleaner, but has been known to top 105 decibels, a thrum equivalent to a chainsaw or ambulance siren. It's the male who makes the noise, by rubbing or stridulating his penis against his abdomen, an unusual trick that has earned him not only the boast of 'loudest animal on Earth relative to body size' but also the Guinness World Record for the planet's 'loudest penis'. Because this remarkable bug plays its song underwater, most of the sound is absorbed, but sit by the edge of a pond or stream in late twilight and you might just hear its grasshopper-like chirps swell into the night air.

The barn swallows have been back for about a month, after their epic flight from South Africa. I'll see them skimming the pond at early dusk, snapping up insects that hang about over its surface or emerge from the lily pads. Occasionally, it looks as if the swallows misjudge their swoops and nudge the surface, creating a splosh of small droplets. Folklore had it that splashing swallows meant rain was surely on the way, but it turns out they're deliberately bathing on the wing, a perilous habit that involves dipping briefly into the pond and flicking a spray of water over their backs.

As twilight darkens, the secretive daubenton's bat occasionally makes itself known. It flies dizzyingly fast, dangerously close to the surface of the pond like a cross-channel hovercraft. This high-risk skimming reaps ample rewards and our countryside's most capable 'water bat' will stuff itself with emerging caddisflies and midges. While many bats flirt with hunting insects over water, none is quite so daring as the daubenton's. Even if it does make a mistake and finds itself landing in the water, this seaplane of a bat will quickly recover and pull itself out of trouble. It also only needs a brief crepuscular window – no more than an hour – to eat half its body weight before returning to its roost.

In just a few weeks from now, the pond will start to whirr with dragonflies. With their lightning-quick, stop-start swoops, it can be almost impossible to identify which sort of dragonfly is looping-the-loop across the top of the water lilies. One species, however, is an absolute whopper, a flying wax crayon of an insect, and will often leave the confines of the water at dusk and race down the woodland ride or along the scraggy hedgerow that separates our fields from the neighbouring farm's. It's called a brown hawker. There are several species of hawker dragonflies, all large and pleasingly chunky. The brown hawker's milk-chocolate body is as long as my index finger, and its wingspan even longer. While it doesn't have the all-over iridescent blue sparkle of its cousin, the emperor hawker, it's still a handsome dragonfly. Its lace-thin wings are burnished with bronze, and the males have a cinched waist and tiny blue spots, like turquoise set into precious metal.

It also has huge, gorgeous eyes, like a fighter pilot's goggles, and a combative temperament to match. An avid entomologist, raking around his favourite Cheshire dragonfly haunts in the late nineteenth century, reserved particular admiration for the fearless brown hawker: 'Hold him by the wings,' he scribbled, 'and he will coolly bite anything from a nail down to cotton-wool [...] I have frequently tried his biting powers, but my epidermis always turns his mandibles; and I have not yet persuaded anyone thinner skinned to submit to the experiment.'[1] Our insect-loving writer also spotted, unusually for a dragonfly, that the brown hawker happily extends its departures well into dusk and skirts well beyond the limits of its home pond. Towards the end of one summer, at 8.30 in the evening, he 'saw one hawking along a hedge in the deep twilight of a still, warm

August night [...] The rising moon was just above the horizon, showing its light on the fleecy clouds and on the white mist hanging over the meadows.'

All species of hawkers are named after their bird-of-prey-like hunting style and the brown hawker is notoriously protective of its territory. It's perhaps not surprising, however, that a dragonfly should defend its patch with energy. The brown hawker, and indeed all dragonflies, rely solely and exclusively on one pond for their every need. As an egg, it will spend the first few weeks of its life close to the water's surface, hidden by its mother inside a reed or piece of rotten wood. The young dragonfly will then spend an inordinately long time as an ugly duckling, in a non-descript larval stage, patrolling the murky waters devouring almost anything smaller than itself, including freshly minted tadpoles and fish fry. After two, three or even four long years, under the cover of darkness the larva will finally transform from pond critter into magnificent flying machine, an overnight metamorphosis that is both rapid and extraordinary. Only when the day length and temperature are just right, in the first few weeks of early summer, will the brown hawker larva begin its transformation. As soon as the evening's darkness falls, the creature will drag itself onto the pond's margins and begin to force a new head, legs and wings out of its thin carapace. It'll take three or four hours of night-time struggles for a glimmering dragonfly to fully emerge, its new soft body and wings slowly hardening in the morning's astronomical and nautical twilight. And, while most new dragonflies or 'tenerals' will wait until after sunrise to take their maiden flight, the brown hawker ventures out for the first time in morning's civil twilight. That way, he or she steals the lead and hopes to avoid becoming breakfast for a hobby falcon, a bird with a particular preference for dragonflies.

As cold-blooded creatures, tadpoles always seek the warmth. As a late spring day ends, they'll wrestle near the pond's surface, hoping to glean some of the Sun's gentle last rays. It takes about four months for the tadpole to transform from frogspawn to tiny frog, and it's a lottery who will make it. We have a resident grey heron who seems to spend most of the year skirting around the pond, hunting principally at dusk and dawn. He or she often stands motionless by the water, head drawn back between its shoulders, only launching into a stately, measured flight, legs trailing behind, if we approach the pond. In late spring, more grey herons arrive, clearly drawn to the seasonal platter of amphibians. A more recent addition has also been a small cattle egret, a bird that looks like a miniature white heron. By day, it haunts the cows on the pasture fields, hoping to snaffle insects that are stirred up by their hooves or drawn to the steaming dung. At dusk and dawn, however, the egret joins the grey herons' sentinel positions next to the water. All stand and wait for tadpoles and baby froglets to float carelessly close to the edge.

A late morning circuit of the pond at frog breeding time will also find its margins littered with macabre remnants of a dusk or dawn raid – frogs' legs, entrails, even dollops of unfertilised frogs' eggs. The last of these swells on contact with moisture from damp grass or early morning drizzle, turning into clumps of amphibian wallpaper paste. For hundreds of years, people were puzzled by these gelatinous piles that seemed to land overnight and called it 'star shot' or 'star blubber', believing it to have fallen from the sky. Some scientists thought it was a strange dusk fungus that grew exponentially overnight, while others believed it to be the remains of earthworms vomited up by 'coddy moddies' or young gulls.[2] One idea even suggested that frogs, caught out in sudden dawn frost, exploded like grenades, leaving behind only mysterious gobs of jelly. As one account in an 1810 edition of the *Encyclopaedia Britannica* revealed: 'The time we always meet with it is after a very wet night, when the air in the morning suddenly clears up, and a sharp frost ensues. The frogs that then happen to be out are immediately seized by the frost, and turned into this jelly-like substance. For as I have had occasion sometimes to go out very early, I have found several parts of the frog not yet dissolved among the jelly, such as feet, legs, and thighs.'[3] The truth, although no less devastating for the frog, is that birds of all kinds — crows, herons, egrets, gulls and magpies — will happily wait in the gloom to skewer amphibians heading to the water's edge. It is the remains of these murderous encounters, with their battlefield brutality, that leave piles of unfertilised frog spawn and spare limbs scattered around my otherwise calm pond.

Under the blanket of deep twilight, it is amazing to think that any of the frogs and toads can find each other. Fascinating research about amphibians has uncovered that many live in a brightly coloured, glow-in-the-dark world that we humans simply can't see. Glow-worms and fireflies 'bioluminesce' — they create light through chemical reactions in their own bodies. Plenty of ocean creatures also produce their own light, as we'll see in the next chapter.

But there is another way you can glow in the dark – biofluorescence. This is where an organism absorbs light at one wavelength, or colour, and then emits it at a different wavelength. And amphibians seem to be particularly good at it. At dusk, when plenty of frogs and toads are out and about, their bodies absorb the deep blue light of twilight and the last scraps of the day's UV light. This is then re-emitted as a different colour – usually reds, oranges or greens. Humans can't see this extraordinary display with the naked eye but fellow amphibians almost certainly can; the only way we can get a sense of all this exuberance and colour is to look at these amazing creatures under special artificial lights. And, it seems, even the dullest amphibians are hiding technicolour clothing. From brightly coloured bellies to polka-dot spots, glowing genitals to luminous urine, many different species of amphibian are employing their glow-in-the-dark skills to attract mates, repel predators and signal to their own kind or other species. In fact, the more research that delves into the world of biofluorescence, the more widespread a phenomenon it seems to be, especially among crepuscular animals or plants that need to attract twilight visitors.

If you care to take a UV light into your garden or on a woodland walk in the dark, a psychedelic world reveals itself. Harvestmen spiders are revealed to be bright purple, slugs' trails fluoresce yellow. Earthworms and compost worms sport turquoise go-faster stripes down their thin bodies, while the dullest moths turn pink and violet. Tree trunks covered in moss and lichen turn brilliant orange; algae that is barely noticeable during the day suddenly shines hot red. Even the flat-leaf parsley, in the herb garden, turns from chlorophyll green to burgundy. Some of our most loved twilight mammals also become technicolour in UV light: researchers have found that dormice show patches of lurid green and purply pink[4] while hedgehogs glow red under UV light.[5] In a rather depressing use of the magical power that is biofluorescence, biotech researchers have recently created tadpoles that glow when something is wrong with their environment. African clawed frog tadpoles have been genetically engineered to biofluoresce green if they have been exposed to chemical contaminants. The hope is that these tadpole scouts, whether they like it or not, will be the first line in detecting toxins in water that disrupt thyroid functioning in humans.[6]

Once frog mating season is over on the smallholding, all but our stalwart heron will abandon ship in search of richer pickings elsewhere. Ours simply stays close by, silently alternating between pond and stubble fields, looking for voles and other small rodents to fill the gap. Whether this year's tadpoles will make it is largely down to the weather; unseasonable cold weather can wreak havoc. And, while some years are noticeably low on tadpole numbers, we have also experienced the other extreme. One balmy early summer followed a very mild spring about five years ago, and an unusually generous amount of baby frogs survived. For two extraordinary days, at dusk, the ground surrounding the pond teemed with biblical numbers of springing, fingernail-sized froglets. Within just a few hours they'd all hopped away into the fields and woodland, an odyssey they'd hopefully go on to repeat, back and forth, year after year.

5

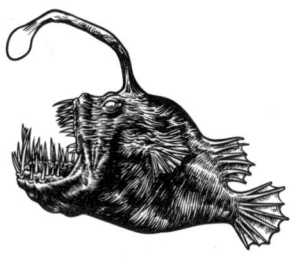

The Greatest Show on Earth

During the Second World War, the US Navy spent weeks hunting the oceans for enemy submarines. Using technology inspired by one of our best-known twilight creatures, the bat, sonic pulses were fired out into the blue depths. Any object or surface these sound waves bounced off would produce an echo, which was picked up by the sonar operator. The amplitude and return time of these 'pings' indicated the distance and size of objects and could be used to create an idea of what, if anything, was lurking below the waves.

What soon became apparent was that something very weird was happening with the ocean bed. Navy sonar operators were deeply puzzled by the fact that the echoes seemed to show that the floor of the sea was moving. During the day, the bottom of the ocean appeared to be about a quarter of a mile down. But, during the night, this seabed shifted and rose upwards, nearer the surface.

Every 24 hours, this pattern was repeated. Come dusk, the seabed rose upwards. Then, at dawn, it would slowly begin to sink back down again.

The existence of this strange 'false bottom' was put down to everything from faulty equipment to sunken islands or shipwrecks interfering with the sonar. Besides, with the war still raging, there was little time or finances to investigate these strange acoustic signals. And so, it wasn't until the end of the conflict, in 1948, that Martin Johnson and fellow scientists at the Scripps Institution of Oceanography could finally investigate and publish the mystery of the shifting seabed. What they discovered, however, was much, much more astonishing. It turned out that what the sonar was picking up wasn't the floor of the ocean. The same signals were also being detected across the globe, in many different places. Moreover, this 'deep scattering layer' – as Johnson called it – was alive.

We now know that what the sonar was picking up was the 'twilight zone' or mesopelagic layer of the ocean (*meso*, middle; *pelagic*, ocean dwelling). It's called the twilight zone for two very good reasons. The first reason is that the levels of light in this remarkable place are not dissimilar to twilight on land. And the second is that truly extraordinary things happen in this inky layer at both dusk and dawn.

The depths of the sea are divided by oceanographers into five layers, like a lasagne. At the very bottom are the trenches that slice deep into the ocean bed. Named after Hades, the god of the underworld, this is the hadal zone. Above this are the abyssal and midnight zones. All three of these deep-sea layers are regions of intense pressure and perpetual, black-night darkness. As you travel through each layer, it also gets colder and less hospitable to life the deeper you sink. At the dappled surface of the ocean, by contrast, is the sunlight zone or epipelagic region, a slim, 200-metre-deep layer where daylight easily penetrates and can support photosynthesis. And, just as terrestrial twilight lies between day and night, so too the ocean's twilight zone – which stretches from 200 metres to 1 kilometre below the surface – sits between light and total darkness and is characterised by the softest wisps of residual light. Here, it is a perpetual, deep dusk.

Just 1 per cent of the Sun's illumination reaches the marine twilight zone but it's enough to support an entire ecosystem from minuscule bacteria to octopus and squid. This extraordinary region contains trillions of life forms perfectly adapted to low light. It's also a place where fairytale creatures reign. From flittering sea angels to monstrous fangtooth fish, vampire squids to glowing siphonophores, linked together in long, living chains – beautiful oddness defines the twilight zone's residents.

In this watery gloaming, the ocean's twilight creatures have evolved spectacular strategies and physical quirks to cope in the tenebrous depths. As with glow-worms and fireflies on dry land, many of the sea's dusk dwellers rely on bioluminescence, the ability to produce their own light source, for hunting, mating and camouflage. The variety and sheer strangeness is breathtaking. Certain kinds of single-celled algae, for example, produce a blue glow when under threat from a predator. This reaction, which is called 'burglar alarm bioluminescence', is designed to illuminate the attacker, like a search light, making the predator vulnerable to being caught by a beast even more deadly than itself. The fire-breathing shrimp, by contrast, uses its bioluminescent gifts like a pepper spray. Under attack, it spews glowing clouds of chemicals from its mouth into the water around it, blinding and confusing the hunter and giving the shrimp a chance to make a hasty exit. Some bioluminescent animals, such as brittle stars, can even eject body parts in the attempt to create a distraction. When under attack, this delicate, long-limbed invertebrate will jettison one of its glowing arms in the hope that the predator will follow the phantom limb, leaving the rest of the brittle star to sneak away into the gloom.

New discoveries are being made by ocean explorers on an almost weekly basis. These natural creations are of such imaginative Jim Henson-like peculiarity that almost anything seems possible. And some of them are also just downright funny. The pigbutt worm, for example, defies belief. The size and shape of a chickpea, this spherical worm looks alarmingly similar to a tiny floating backside. Commonly known in oceanography circles as 'flying buttocks', this diminutive creature lives at the lowest levels of the twilight zone, where it feeds on organic debris. It is also bioluminescent in two ways. When agitated, it produces a bright blue light that lasts for up to six seconds. As a secondary form of defence, it also emits a green glowing puff of particles from the crack in its bottom-like body, leading one BBC science journalist to dub it the 'worm whose farts glow green'.[1]

Other twilight sea creatures use their bioluminescence as a lure. The female anglerfish, for example, dangles a glowing lobe from her forehead, like a luminous fishing-fly on the end of a line. This lustrous orb flashes with blue-green light, an allure that is apparently almost impossible to resist if you are a shrimp or small fry. What's even more curious is that the glow isn't produced by the anglerfish, but by a helpful team of bioluminescent bacteria that live on its host's bauble-like appendage. And, rather than just glow all the time, like an annoying light you can't switch off, the anglerfish somehow communicates with her bacterial colleagues and tells them when to start shining. In return, the bacteria get nutrients from the fish and a safe place to live.

The anglerfish's bright lure isn't just used for finding food in the shadows. In the vast, dimly lit ocean, finding a mate can be hard work, especially if there aren't many suitable partners in the vicinity. When scientists first studied certain species of anglerfish they were bemused by the fact that they only ever seemed to find females, although many had what appeared to be parasites attached to their bodies. Further research revealed that these unsightly appendages turned out to be male anglerfish, firmly embedded into their mates. Anglerfish can range in length from the tiddly (2 centimetres) to the monstrous (a metre), with females often outsizing their mates. One species of anglerfish found in the twilight zone (*Oneirodes eschrichtii*) takes this sexual dimorphism to its extremes, with the male being only a wee golf ball to his football-sized lover. Drawn by the light of a female, and her chemical scent, the male will become immediately attached. Literally. Using his tiny sharp teeth, he'll bite into her side and start to fuse his body with hers. Soon, his head will have dissolved, his blood supply will join her own, and he'll become little more than a sperm bank. His ability to provide a constant supply of sperm, however, is ingenious in such unforgiving surroundings. It means that the female will never again have to scour the dimly lit depths for a mate, and all her eggs, from that point on, will be fertile. And while it's a permanent, binding union, one that will only end when the female dies, it isn't always exclusive. Female anglerfish are known to carry up to eight mates at any one time, a polyamorous twilight romance if there ever was one.

In the low ambient light levels of the twilight layer, another problem presents itself. Viewed from underneath, anything moving through the sea creates a clear silhouette against the brighter-lit water above. And so, some animals have evolved an ingenious cloaking device, using bioluminescent spots on their downward-facing surfaces. This shimmering surface reduces the contrast between the creature and the surrounding water, helping them to blend into their surroundings and move around undetected. Even as light levels change, thanks to the passing of the day or the Sun going behind a cloud, many bioluminescent creatures can adjust their brightness, like a dimmer switch, keeping them veiled from predators. The thumb-sized marine hatchet fish, for instance, has rows of glowing pale blue lights along its thin, flat-as-a-pancake belly. These match the daylight filtering down from above and mask the creature's silhouette from below. Sadly, the hatchet fish's invisibility shroud doesn't fool everyone and some of the twilight zone's creatures have developed ways of seeing through the trick. The barrel-eye fish, for example, has evolved special proteins in its eyes that allow it to see through any bioluminescent cloaking. The barrel-eye fish is also perfectly designed for half-light skulking; living at the very bottom of the twilight zone, nearly 1 kilometre down, it has eyes that almost permanently point upwards, through the top of its transparent head, scanning for shadowy shapes in the waters above.

The cookie-cutter shark also takes advantage of counterillumination, but in an incredibly Machiavellian way. This relatively small shark, which rarely exceeds lengths of half a metre, more than makes up for its size with a clever piece of deception. Like many twilight creatures whose undersides glow, to hide them from being seen from below, the cookie-cutter's belly can produce a green glow that camouflages its body. Crucially, however, the cookie-cutter leaves a band around its neck unlit. When viewed from below, this sneaky shark's collar is mistaken for the outline of a small fish, encouraging other predators to attack. Only once the predator has got too close will the cookie-cutter spring its own surprise and launch a much more deadly counterattack. With its sucker-like lips and bandsaw-sharp teeth, it attaches itself to its victim and then spins around, cutting out a biscuit-shaped plug of flesh. Size seems to be absolutely no barrier to a cookie-cutter attack. Scientists have found the bodies of yellow-fin tuna, seals, killer whales and even great white sharks with the cookie-cutter-sized chunks removed from their bodies.

Lots of the twilight zone's animals have evolved remarkable ways of seeing in the dim light. This steel-blue layer of the ocean is home to plenty of creatures, for example, that have evolved enormous eyes to compensate for low levels of illumination. As light travels from the Sun and hits the ocean, its light waves will carry on travelling below the surface of the water. Water molecules, however, absorb red light more strongly than blue light. This means that red light waves won't reach depths of any further than about 10 metres, yellow light penetrates to around 30 metres, and green light can get to about 60 metres. Blue light can travel the furthest, to 75 metres and beyond. Even at the lowest reaches of the twilight zone, blue light penetrates, albeit in minute quantities.

The bigger the eye, the greater the ability to capture the few photons of light that do make it down to the deepest levels of the twilight zone. The colossal squid, for example, has the largest animal eyes ever studied at nearly 30 centimetres across, about the size of a dinner plate, with 9-centimetre pupils – so large you could fit your hand through them. These huge eyes, which are three times bigger even than those belonging to blue whales, are optimised for spotting their most feared predator – the sperm whale – up to 120 metres away. The colossal squid's football-like eyes can't see the sperm whale itself but rather they detect the clouds of bioluminescent plankton that swirl and roll in the sperm whale's wake. Detecting these glowing billows, at a distance just on the limits of the sperm whale's sonar range, allows the squid to take evasive action and escape undetected.

Another amazing set of twilight-adapted eyes belongs to the cock-eyed squid, a rather unkind name for a very pretty, strawberry-pink cephalopod. It does have, nevertheless, the rather unusual feature of having one eye noticeably larger and more bulging than the other. As it moves through the dark water, in gentle and slow balletic turns, its large eye looks upwards while the smaller eye looks down towards the ocean floor. Research has revealed these mis-matched eyes are perfectly suited for hunting in the twilight zone – the larger eye is designed for spotting prey from underneath, its increased size allowing it to capture as much downwelling light as possible.[2] This large eye also has a yellow lens, which acts like a magic monocle, and sees right through other creatures' counterillumination disguises. With the cock-eyed squid's big eye scanning the water above for supper, its little eye can concentrate on what's happening below. Designed to pick up different visual signals, the cock-eyed squid's smaller eye patrols the waters beneath, using its wide field of vision to look for signs of bioluminescent life.

The twilight zone is also an apt name for this little-known ecosystem because, every day, at dawn and dusk, an incredible journey takes place. As we already know, at the very surface of the ocean is the 'sunlight zone'. Here, in this upper layer, the Sun's rays easily penetrate the seawater and tiny plants called phytoplankton thrive. Phytoplankton also happens to be the favourite food of hordes of small sea creatures that live in the twilight zone, from zooplankton to jellyfish and fish. The only problem is that the sunlight zone is also patrolled by avid hunters – seabirds, whales and bigger fish – who often hunt by sight in the daylight. And so, in the world's biggest game of hide-and-seek, creatures in the twilight zone wait until after sunset before heading up, en masse, in a vertical migration to the sunlight zone. Only then, under the cover of failing light, they can gorge on phytoplankton while trying to avoid the risk of being someone else's supper. As daybreak arrives, and the daylight dangers re-emerge, the creatures of the twilight zone swim back down to the safety of the opaque depths, bellies full.

Billions upon billions of marine animals, twice a day, make this incredible journey at dusk and dawn. It is Earth's largest animal migration and one that most people have never even heard of. Back in the 1840s, naturalist Edward Forbes had proposed what went on to be a widely accepted theory that few creatures could live in the gloomy depths of the ocean. In fact, according to Forbes's 'Abyssus theory', marine life would be impossible beyond 300 fathoms, about 550 metres below the surface, given this region's eternal murkiness and enormous pressure. It took the tenacity and risk-taking of scientists aboard the German Valdivia Expedition, led by marine biologist Carl Chun, at the end of the 1890s to challenge Forbes's theory and show that a carnival of extraordinary life lived deep underwater. Science could barely believe the creatures the expedition caught from the depths. Perhaps the most famous was the vampire squid, a dark-cloaked, soft-bodied cephalopod that could turn itself inside out to avoid predators. Dramatically named *Vampyroteuthis infernalis* – the 'Vampire from Hell' – this rugby ball of a creature is actually a sweetie, a gentle sifter of organic debris rather than a fanged terror of the deep. The squid and other twilight dwellers, nevertheless, caught the world's imagination and revealed an entire and wonderful ecosystem below 300 fathoms.

With such remarkable discoveries, Forbes's idea could no longer hold water. Despite the scientific community having more than a century to explore the ocean's depths since the Valdivia Expedition, the difficulties and cost of deep-sea exploration have meant that the twilight zone is still full of mystery. A paper published in 2014[3] suggested that the scientific and fishing community had hugely underestimated the sheer scale of life in the mesopelagic layer, and that there could be more fish in the twilight zone than in the rest of the ocean combined. Lantern fish, for example, are one of the layer's most abundant creatures and we are only just beginning to learn how important they are. Named after the bioluminescent markings on their bellies, there are nearly 250 species of lantern fish which, together, constitute an astonishing volume of fish. Thought to have a global biomass of up to 16 gigatonnes (the equivalent of 3.2 billion African elephants), lantern fish are so staggeringly numerous that if estimations about its population size are correct, this little-understood animal is one of the most abundant, and hidden, vertebrates in the world.

Creatures in the twilight zone are intensely sensitive to changes in the amount of light that penetrates the mesopelagic layer. So much so, that even close to the Arctic, when polar winter means weeks of permanent, deep blue twilight, creatures bobbing around in the mesopelagic zone can still detect tiny changes in light intensity, enough to keep their body clocks in rhythm and maintain their dusk visits to the surface. Researchers who spent a long, frosty spell in the Svalbard archipelago, between Norway and the North Pole, used underwater recordings to monitor the daily vertical migrations of krill. Their findings showed that these tiny shrimp-like crustaceans seem to be able to sense microscopically subtle changes in the sky's changing light levels as the

Sun shifted its position below the horizon.[4] Their twice-daily twilight migrations carried on.

Many top predators, like marine mammals, seabirds, and even some of the fish we eat, rely on creatures from the twilight zone for their meals. Swordfish, for example, take the same daily commute as many other twilight creatures but are not on the hunt for phytoplankton. During the day, they stick to the deeper waters of the mesopelagic layer, hoping to avoid predators. After sundown, they follow the twilight crowds to the surface only to dine out on fellow commuters, such as small fish and squid. Other predators, who spend much of their time in the warmer, sunlight layer, take regular deep dives into the twilight zone during the day to catch the creatures hiding there. Tuna, for instance, get about two-thirds of their food, including squid and lantern fish, from this hidden, near-dark world.

The ocean's twilight zone is a supercontinent of teeming animation. It's also, it turns out, entirely critical to the continuation of life on Earth. All the small creatures who tirelessly travel up to the surface and back down again are providing an invaluable service to the carbon cycle. Carbon dioxide (CO_2) is captured from the atmosphere by phytoplankton, near the ocean's surface, during photosynthesis. The phytoplankton is then, in turn, eaten by the creatures of the twilight zone, whose daily migrations drag the carbon further down into the depths of the ocean. When these twilight zone animals poo, get eaten by something else, or die, the resulting carbon-rich material – known as 'marine snow' – also sinks further into the depths. The whole process is a vital component of the ocean's ability to capture carbon from the air and trap it deep underwater. Scientists estimate that about 90 per cent of all the carbon that is dragged into the twilight zone by marine life stays there, with a small percentage sinking even further down into the darker realms, or settling on the ocean's floor or in its trenches, where it will remain safely trapped underwater for hundreds or even thousands of years. Current estimates suggest the oceans absorb about a quarter of the world's entire carbon emissions, a twilight miracle if there ever was.

Twilight Diary

Autumn

I have been glued to the skies for over a month. Late autumn has put on quite the show, week after week of strikingly beautiful dawns and blazing dusks. In October, the rising of the Sun is wonderfully delayed and civil twilight doesn't start until about half past six in the morning, just the time when I'm getting dressed and can watch the spectacle unfold through my bedroom's tall sash window. Every morning is different. And, apart from the odd washout, when lashing rain spoils the entire day, most dawns at this time of year are astonishing. It's a light show in slow motion, one that subtly changes with every minute that passes, and many of the morning's twilights are heavy with mist. Looking out over the wide expanse of the valley bottom, the view from our old farmhouse faces entirely south and offers a 180-degree panorama of indefinable loveliness. The turquoise-green fields and outlines of trees are almost swallowed by a low fog that lingers well until after sunrise but adds an air of trickery to the strangeness of first light. To the east, however, a dawn fire has been lit behind the hill. It's intensely orange and hot red, but burns low to the skyline, its source still hidden from view. This bed of embers spreads its warmth, lighting up the cotton wool stratocumulus clouds that sit above it. Between the clouds, the pale blue upper reaches of the sky peek through, although to the west it is as if time hasn't caught up. There, beyond the copse, it might as well still be dark.

October evening twilight is just as gorgeous. The best moment of evening's twilight is usually around seven o'clock, just as most people are settling down for supper. If I'm still out around the smallholding – grabbing logs from the woodshed or closing barn doors – I'm treated to a thick, treacly twilight. Over in the west, a thin line of gold butters the horizon, topped with a layer of red haze, and it is the turn of the east to be cast in black. And keeping the glow company is often a bright white dot of light, hanging low in the west. It's Venus, a cloud-swaddled planet that burns so hot it is often mistaken for a star. And despite being nearly 150 million kilometres away, it is searchlight bright.

Now, in November, dawn is perhaps at its most cheerfully gaudy, or it certainly has been this year. The combination of a hard, silvery frost and a Fauvist sky – with its vibrant, exaggerated colours – are too flamboyant to ignore. From excitable conversations in the village shop, it is as if we've all never seen dawn before, but these dreamlike mornings just keep coming. At about seven thirty, the sweet spot of mid-civil twilight, the sky is laughably psychedelic – almost volcanic. From east to south – a full quarter of the compass – the morning heavens are a swirling cauldron of extreme reds, white-hot yellows, deep violet clouds and patches of royal blue. For what seems like an impossibly long stretch of skyline, there is a thick volcanic-scarlet band, above which there is an equally deep layer of yolk-yellow. At other times of the year, morning's twilight seems to be a soft wash of colours, one gently bleeding into another, but this month there is no such nicety. Dawn is an absolute riot. And completely unignorable.

This feeling of complete awe at the otherworldly, ever-changing beauty of twilight is no doubt ancient.

Sunrise and sunset, and their sisters dawn and dusk, seem to have held a special significance to many cultures and faiths throughout time. In Islam, dawn and dusk are two of the most important times for prayer and, during Ramadan, fasting begins at morning twilight and ends after sunset. Twilight represents not a dangerous, degraded time but an intermediate zone when prayers are perhaps most likely to be heard. In Judaism, calendar days run from nightfall to nightfall. Shabbat is the Jewish Day of Rest, for example, and begins around sunset on Friday and ends on Saturday evening, when the Sun is 8 degrees below the horizon. Other signs are also watched for, to know when Shabbat should end, including the appearance of three stars in the sky and the disappearance of any traces of red twilight in the western sky. In Christianity, religious festivals also often begin after sunset on the evening before the holy day. The Early Church carried on the Jewish practice of starting the calendar day at dusk, which is why we still celebrate Christmas Eve and the Easter Vigil after twilight has arrived.

This idea that the day starts with the setting of the Sun, rather than its rise, is curious. Its pedigree is longstanding: writing about the Gauls, the Celtic tribes who lived in mainland Europe, Julius Caesar wrote that 'they compute the divisions of every season, not by the number of days, but of nights; they keep birthdays and the beginnings of months and years in such an order that the day follows the night'.[1] The year was also thought to be divided into a light half and a dark half – each new year began with the arrival of darkness at Samhain at the beginning of November. Days began with evening's twilight and ended 24 hours later with the Sun once again disappearing below the horizon. We still count weeks, not in days, but in fortnights (fourteen nights) and, until relatively recently, sennights (seven nights).

So why measure time in nights, from dusk to dusk? Evidence from archaeology has shown that, for thousands of years, our ancestors carefully monitored the motions of the Sun and Moon. Many cultures had solar and lunar deities – from the Egyptians to the Vikings, the Aztecs to ancient Chinese – and took a close interest in the skies. Survival, whether you are hunter-gatherers, pastoralists or farming communities, depended heavily on knowing where you were in the yearly cycle. Understanding the rhythms and timings of the year allowed a community to be efficient, keep track of time, plan ahead, plant and harvest, and make use of seasonal bounties. Rather than simply wake up every day and look to the weather as a guide – which can be hugely variable, especially in higher latitudes – watching the cycles of the Moon and the Sun's rising and setting points on the horizon gave a much more accurate picture of the year's progression.

Two particular events acted as key markers in the year. The two solstices are the longest and shortest days, usually around 21 June and 21 December respectively. At the summer solstice in Yorkshire this year, for example, the Sun shone for over 15 hours; at the winter solstice, it appeared for less than seven and a half. Throughout time, these special days have taken on a distinctive meaning, one encoded in monuments and artefacts to be used at special rituals and social gatherings.

Perhaps the most well-known of these monuments is Stonehenge, arguably the Western world's most famous stone circle. Its huge sarsen stones, and smaller blue stones, which were heaved into place around 2500 BCE, were carefully arranged to line up with the movements of the Sun. These enormous blocks were arranged with remarkable precision to frame the sunrise at midsummer solstice and the midwinter solstice sunset. Standing in the middle of the monument, it would have been impossible to miss the immense significance of these two transitional moments in the solar calendar. And, far from Stonehenge being the only place where these events were witnessed and celebrated, it seems as if the surrounding landscape was also part of the ritual. Woodhenge, a monument close by, also aligns with the midwinter and midsummer solstices. At nearby Durrington Wells – where the men and women who built Stonehenge are believed to have lived – there is another circular monument known as the Southern Circle. This, unlike Stonehenge, is orientated towards the midwinter sunrise and archaeologists are now starting to piece together a picture of a dynamic landscape, one where people would have stood in the Southern Circle at dawn, waiting for the winter Sun to rise, before slowly processing to Stonehenge for the midwinter sunset. Mass slaughter of livestock and subsequent feasting, riotous celebrations, and the coming together of different, far-flung groups would have been part of the festivities to mark the turning point of the year. Other elaborate monuments from this time also appear to align with solstice sunrises and sunsets, including prehistoric sites in Orkney, Meath in Ireland, and Anglesey, Wales. The more we learn about Stonehenge and similar prehistoric temples, the more it becomes clear that these places were not sites of brief occupation but rather built, rebuilt, extended and altered over multiple generations.

Across the world, there are many other examples. In Portugal and Spain, for example, there are 177 monuments called Seven-stone Antas. They're mini megaliths — six big stones propped up to create a small room-size chamber, roofed with another large stone — and all of them are aligned to frame sunrise on the horizon at certain times of the year.[2] In Egypt, a number of ancient buildings, including the Temple of Amun at Karnak, which was built around 2000 BCE, were carefully constructed to frame the dawn at the winter solstice. And some ancient complexes, such as Chankillo in Peru, were even built as huge calendars on the landscape. There, a neat row of thirteen stone towers, constructed along the ridge of a hill around 250–200 BCE, helped the people who built it mark the daily rising and setting arcs of the Sun. Armed with this information, the community could know when to expect not only the solstices and two equinoxes (when day and night are of equal length) but also where they were in the year to an accuracy of within one or two days.[3]

*

AUTUMN

Not too far from the smallholding, in Yorkshire, are the Thornborough Henges. This extraordinary triple-henge monument is considered the 'Stonehenge of the North', and yet few people, even fellow Yorkshire dwellers, have even heard of it. Extending for more than a mile, the monument consists of three huge circular enclosures, their walls made from banked earth, linked together with a straight, wide avenue. The circular enclosures – each one with a diameter of nearly 250 metres – had entrances and exits on opposing sides. When they were built around 3000 BCE, the perimeter banks of earth were so high that anyone inside any of the enclosures would have only been able to see the sky above, apart from the views allowed through the access points. They were also covered with white gypsum dug from the surrounding land, a technique that would have given the monuments a shimmering glow.

The entire monument is orientated along roughly a north-west, south-east axis. Computer models which mimic the evening sky above the Thornborough Henges around the time of their construction reveal that the central circular enclosure, or henge, aligns with the midwinter solstice. The whole complex, however, also seems to be orientated towards the rising of Orion's Belt — and other single bright stars — at the winter solstice. As the Earth revolves around the Sun, this creates the different views of the evening sky — stars can be as seasonal as the Sun's movements, appearing and reappearing with the passing months. Archaeologists are now starting to wonder whether the horizon, and its relationship with both the Sun and the stars, may have been at the heart of our most ancient structures. The skyline was, perhaps, 'the mediator between the skyscape and the landscape, between the earth and sky'.[4] In fact, a whole new field of study — called horizon astronomy — delves deep into this idea that transitional times of the day and year, including twilight, are deeply embedded in our oldest cultures.

It's revealing to discover that, underneath the Thornborough Henges, there is another even older sky-watching monument. This is a cursus, a long, rectangular 44-metre-wide enclosure that stretched for at least three quarters of a mile. Built only a few years after the first Neolithic farmers arrived in this country, around 3600 BCE, this monument also appears to be aligned with the midwinter solstice. The A1(M) road now skirts around the Thornborough Henge complex. Few people, as they speed past, realise that they are travelling through a landscape changed by people who moved mountains to capture special moments on the horizon.

The few hunter-gatherers who lived lightly on the land around North Yorkshire, in the long stretch of time before the arrival of Thornborough's Neolithic farmers, left nothing to tell us about how they viewed dawn and dusk. In fact, across continents, scholars argue with great passion about whether hunter-gatherer societies of the past even bothered to monitor, with any precision, what was happening in the sky. And still, there are some exciting clues that suggest even in the Upper Palaeolithic period in Europe (roughly 50,000 to 12,000 BCE) some groups of people were acutely aware of the changing patterns of sunset and sunrise during the year. A number of famous Palaeolithic caves, those adorned with painted images, seem to have been chosen because their entrances were illuminated by the setting or rising Sun at the solstices. The French rock shelters in Lascaux and Bernifal, for example, are only lit up by the setting Sun at the summer solstice. Another French cave, Abri Castanet, is filled with sunset light at the winter solstice.

Archaeologists are rightly cautious to use modern-day hunter-gatherer societies as a proxy for prehistoric groups, but that doesn't mean studying twenty-first-century foraging and hunting communities can't offer some insights into how people might have viewed the world in the past. A study published in the *Cambridge Archaeological Journal*, one that collected information on over eighty extant hunter-gatherer societies, found that most of them closely observed patterns of dawn and dusk through the year. Moreover, the appearance of the winter solstice in particular set into motion numerous rituals, dances, feasts and, in some cases, periods of food restrictions. The people in the groups who monitored the movements of the Sun, and the changing twilight times of the year, were also often regarded as 'special' and were shamans, priests or elders. Those who had the role of 'calendar expert' also held power – they were the ones who decided when important ceremonies, feasting and dances would begin. In the Quinault culture of North America, for example, it is the 'old men' who are charged with observing both sunrise and sunset every day. Watching from the same location – usually a pole placed in the ground or a designated tree or rock – they count time in dusks and dawns.[5]

Between then and now, our relationship with twilight has been one of close association. Throughout time, both dusk and dawn have been so important that they were embodied in mythologies across the world. In European and Central Asian culture, for example, beliefs in a dawn goddess can be seen through the ages, and people who study comparative mythologies see clear links between cultures who shared similar beliefs. Nomadic herders, who occupied the steppes from Eastern Europe to Central Asia from as early as 6000 BCE, are thought to have believed in a dawn goddess – Hausos – a name meaning to glow red or shine. From these early beginnings, we see similar dawn goddesses emerge as these various peoples travelled, traded and settled across Eurasia over subsequent generations. From the Greek goddess Eos to ancient Rome's Aurora, the Anglo-Saxon goddess Eostre to Usha in Hinduism and Azume in Japanese Shinto, all these different deities of morning twilight probably share a common lineage back to Hausos. Many of these dawn goddesses also have mirror-image partners – gods of evening twilight. The Greek goddess of dawn, Eos, for example, is married to Astraeus, god of dusk, and together their harmonious union symbolised the perpetual dance between day and night. Every morning, Eos was said to rise from the warm embrace of her husband and begin filling the sky with the glorious reds and golden hues of dawn. From there she journeys across the sky, until dusk, when she is reunited with her beloved. And, unlike many of the combative Greek gods, Astraeus is depicted as introspective and serene, the perfect qualities of a contemplative dusk.

Sometimes dawn and dusk are represented as sisters, wives or dual incarnations. In the ancient Hindu festival of Chhath, a celebration of the Sun and its life-giving properties, worshippers celebrate both Usha (goddess of dawn) and Pratyusha (goddess of dusk), both wives of the sun god Surya. In Egyptian mythology, Hathor was a goddess associated with the dawning sky. Each day, she gave birth to the Sun. Often depicted as a cow, a revered symbol of motherhood and nourishment, Hathor birthed the Sun as a golden calf – the red streaks of dawn were said to be the blood of her daily labours.[6] Canaanites – people who lived in the Near East more than three thousand years ago – also celebrated their own dawn and dusk 'twins'. Their half-light gods Shahar (dawn) and Shalem (dusk) were half-brothers, children born of the same father – El, the creator god – but different mothers. They were a divine, inseparable pair and a symbol of the peaceful passing of the day. Shalem is thought to have been such an important god that some scholars believe that Jerusalem may have been named after him – the city of the dusk god.

Remarkably, the moment we seemed to most appreciate twilight was just before we lost it. The Victorians and Edwardians were obsessed with dusk and dawn, its meanings and its romance. Twilight wasn't simply a time of day, for many it also represented a feeling or mood. While the daylight hours were for work and public life, and night-time was swallowed by sleep, twilight was synonymous with home and its comforts. As one anonymous nineteenth-century writer, contributing to Dublin University's magazine, so perfectly captured: 'Gathered now and then out of the common round of daily life at home, come twilight times, between work and rest, when evening seems to pause a moment before passing into the night, and we take thankfully the quiet gloaming with its shadows and seclusion.' Twilight, and its strangely comforting half-light, allowed people a brief moment of respite from the pressures of growing industry, social conventions and duty. At home, in front of the fire or sitting in a comfortable armchair, one could truly be themselves. Evening twilight was also a time for recuperation and a reminder of the more important things in life, the quiet shadowiness of the hour adding to its power: 'Kind words spoken in the twilight, music in the twilight, meditation in the twilight, each have a peculiar power. In the gleamy yet shadowy twilight we near the spirit land.'[7]

For our Victorian author, there was clearly beauty and poetry in this strange period of time. He was no doubt wrestling with the effects of a world industrialising before his very eyes, or the constant demands of city life, but there is something timeless in his sentiment. Life cannot just consist of either being full speed or fast asleep – the transitional, quiet times are arguably the most important. They're the moments when shoulders relax, thoughts unwind and true intimacy resides. Or, as our world-weary writer put it: 'A beautiful face is never more lovely than when seen with the under fire-glow gleaming softly yet richly upon it. In such intervals of rest there is a peculiar homeliness and comfort, largely enjoyable as a contrast to possible vexations, and forced interviews with uncongenial or grasping people during the day.'

There was also a sense that the twilight, especially dusk, was a time when important ideas and thoughts started to germinate. 'It is the hour when greatness, yet inchoate and undeveloped, grows within its husk — the seedtime of future excellence through fermentation of thought,' wrote publisher and politician William Chambers, in 1878, the last years of his life. He was besotted with twilight, and all its meanings, not least how dusk seemed to be the time when creativity and ambition were at their greatest:

> The gloaming is the hour of the highest thoughts of which we may be capable; the hour when the poet sings his song in his own heart before he has written down the words on paper; when the painter sees his picture completed by the divine artistry of the imagination before he has set his palette or sketched in the outline; when the un-formed and chaotic thought long floating in the brain, clears itself from the mists and takes definite shape.[8]

Nearly an octogenarian when forming his thoughts about twilight, or 'the gloaming' as he liked to call it, Chambers also pondered the meaning of the phrase 'twilight years'. For him, there was a sense that they represented a kind of wisdom and experience, only gained through the passage of time. To describe the last stage of a person's life in this way was not a crude metaphor about fading away. It was about a quiet strength that came from mature reflection. 'In the gloaming,' he mused, 'the soul seems to see the right value and the true shapes of things more clearly than it did when the sun was high, and the eyes were dazzled with its shine and the blood fevered with its heat.'[9] It was an idea with some heritage. Nearly four hundred years earlier, Shakespeare had expressed his own ideas about the twilight years in Sonnet 73, a piece that reflects on ageing and strengthening love:

> *In me thou see'st the twilight of such day,*
> *As after sunset fadeth in the west,*
> *Which by-and-by black night doth take away,*
> *Death's second self, that seals up all in rest*
> *In me thou see'st the glowing of such fire*
> *That on the ashes of his youth doth lie,*
> *As the death-bed whereon it must expire*
> *Consum'd with that which it was nourish'd by*
> *This thou perceivest, which makes thy love more strong,*
> **To love that well which thou must leave ere long.**

We rarely give ourselves the opportunity to experience the circumspection of twilight. Or allow all its contemplative qualities to wash over us. One of the only ways we can still get close to this feeling is sitting around a campfire, as evening falls, and experiencing what it does to our way of thinking and interacting with others. Without the glaring distractions of modern living, most people including myself instantly sink into another mode. Convivial silence, intimate conversation, meditative focus – we relate to ourselves and others in a completely different way. Our sense of our surroundings also changes. We start to notice the temperature slide as the light falls, and huddle closer to the flames. The air's moisture creeps up, turning dry summer grass wet. The landmarks around us change, from detail to darkness – trees and buildings become silhouettes, and the sky is thrown into light relief. And the sounds of twilight, away from the constant thrum of noise pollution, are pinpoints in the silence – an owl hoot, the rustle of a field mouse, the drumming of pheasant wings. Dawn, by contrast, invites a whole different set of feelings. The air is often so thickly fresh that, regardless of the time of year, I'll throw open the window and draw in deep lungfuls. There is a sense of promise, of opportunity, about morning's twilights – it's the day made new and perfect. The things that give me purpose and pleasure – family, animals, the farm, the garden, writing – are like presents waiting to be unwrapped. If I knew I only had a day to live, it would start with a dawn walk around the farm and end with a dusk campfire.

Dusk and dawn have been part of the human experience for thousands of years. They have shaped our mythologies and monuments, influenced our rituals and provided rich metaphors. Twilight was both a beginning and an end to the day, but also a barrier through which magical things might happen. Beyond its cultural history, however, does it really matter in this modern age if we take any notice of twilight? In our 24-hour artificially illuminated world, where people spend between 80–90 per cent of their entire day indoors according to the UK government,[10] we are often divorced from the natural cues provided by the changing nature of daylight. What exactly do we stand to lose – much more than just this peace – by ignoring twilight and scrubbing its gentle transitions into two stark portions of night and day?

6

Dawn Births, Neanderthal DNA and Upside-Down Moths

For almost the entire span of human history, artificial light couldn't compete with the glorious spectacle that was night, bookended by the two twilights. Early humans probably took advantage of natural fires, such as forest flames or lightning strikes, and tried to keep them alight by adding more fuel. But the ability to make fire and control it seems to have taken longer to evolve, arriving sometime around 120,000 years ago. From then on, we have lived in a world that was gently lit by campfires and, sometime after 50,000 BCE, the occasional oil lamp. Candles, rushlights, hearths, oil lamps, flame torches - until the advent of gas light in the early nineteenth century, all forms of artificial light were intimate, personal and, with the odd exception, threw out very little illumination beyond their very immediate environment. Twilight remained largely untouched.

By the 1820s, parts of London were aflame with new gas lights, lighting up its theatres and social spaces, but most people's homes still relied on the glow of the hearth and a handful of tapers to see them through the darker hours. Electric lighting followed about half a century later but its spread was dimmed by both poverty and rurality. Indeed, in the UK, after the First World War only one in twenty houses was connected to power.

By the end of the 1940s, thanks to technologies fast-tracked by a world at war for a second time, many homes across Europe and North America were connected to electricity. In the following decades, access to electricity spread around the world but by the 1970s, electric lighting was not only becoming ubiquitous, in some places it was starting to become a problem. The constant glare from bright streetlights, commercial properties, road lighting, traffic headlights, homes, billboards, public buildings, and many other sources was beginning to have an effect on the night sky. Astronomers noticed that it was getting progressively more difficult to see stars and constellations in the night sky – 'light pollution' was spoiling the view. Every year since, the situation has worsened. In fact, it has accelerated. Between 1992 and 2017, light pollution globally has increased exponentially and it is estimated that over 80 per cent of the world's population now live under light-polluted skies.

This matters for many reasons. Naturally dark skies have become so rare they are viewed by many in conservation as of a similar value to clean air, soil and water. Light pollution is also creating unique problems for crepuscular plants and animals, both of which we know are acutely sensitive to even minute changes in the intensity and colour of light. This isn't just a few creatures – biologists estimate that a third of all vertebrates and two-thirds of all invertebrates are particularly vulnerable to artificial light.[1] Practically every animal and plant lovingly described in this book is being damaged by light pollution. Studies have shown unequivocally that artificial light interferes with the fragile twilight relationship between moths, beetles and other evening pollinators, for example, and the plants that rely on them. Crepuscular insects become confused and disorientated by artificial light which, in turn, means plants fail to be pollinated and can't reproduce.[2]

The knowledge that crepuscular insects are irresistibly drawn to light has been around since at least Roman times. The Latin palindrome *In girum imus nocte et consumimur igni*, 'We enter the circle at night and are consumed by fire' – attributed to Virgil – is thought to reference moths' fatal attraction to candlelight. And yet, until very recently, no-one knew why. Lots of theories have been put forward over the years: insects' sensitive eyes are temporarily blinded by bright lights, for example, or moths are lured by the heat that often comes from flames and incandescent bulbs. Researchers at the Department of Bioengineering at Imperial College, London, however, revealed an unexpected and extraordinary explanation.[3] Artificial light - at twilight - is preventing insects from figuring out which way is up. Under natural conditions, insects who fly in dim light rely on minute amounts of light, usually coming from the twilit sky, but also moonlight and starlight, to tell them where the sky is. To fly the right way up, insects usually tilt their bodies so their backs are facing towards wherever the brightest part of their visual field is, i.e. above. Artificial lights - such as streetlamps - disrupt this behaviour and cause insects to turn their backs towards the new, man-made light source instead. Trapped by the disorientating glare of a light bulb, insects will then orbit in endless circles around it - looping-the-loop trying to work out which way is up. Other insects start to pitch up steeply towards the sky before stalling or, even worse, attempting to fly upside down and crashing.

Even plants that aren't pollinated by half-light insects are affected. Light pollution is changing plants' growth and flowering patterns, allowing photosynthesis to happen when a plant should be resting, or encouraging a plant to blossom or set seed too soon. Continuous

24-hour light, for instance, weakens a plant's resistance to disease. This is not only problematic for the plant but for an entire network of biodiversity that relies on it. When temperate trees such as oak and ash are grown next to streetlamps, for instance, their leaves will start growing days earlier than those exposed to natural light/dark cycles. Another study into the effect of streetlights on trees showed that trees which grew near artificial lights that were on between dusk and dawn grew much tougher leaves. This foliage was then less appetising for the insects that normally ate them.[4] This one small change could threaten the entire food chain, including the birds and mammals that rely on the trees and its invertebrates.

Creatures that magically bioluminesce, like our very own glow-worm, simply cannot compete with the glare of bright lights. Female glow-worms, when exposed to light pollution, lose the will to sparkle, limiting their chances to attract a mate.[5] Crepuscular bats are also damaged by artificial light in two ways: not only does it make them easy targets for predators, such as owls, but it also interferes with where they feel safe roosting, hunting and drinking, limiting the places they are able to breed and thrive.[6] Even animals that have adapted well to the busy demands of urban areas, such as hedgehogs, are finding that artificial light is affecting the availability of food. Earthworms, one of the hedgehog's favourite foods, are famously shy of light and at least one study has shown that artificial light reduces their crepuscular and nightly visits to the soil surface by a staggering 75 per cent.[7] Not only does this mean the earthworms won't be doing all the things that earthworms do under the cover of dim light – mating, eating, pulling precious organic material into the soil to improve it – they're also not making themselves available to be hedgehog food or a meal for the many other twilight creatures – including foxes, badgers, wild boar, frogs, toads and weasels.

Amphibians, which are at their most active in the half-light, are sent into disarray by artificial light. Excessive lighting at the twilight times when many frogs, toads and newts are out and about interferes with almost every facet of their lives from sexual development to tadpole growth. It also takes amphibians a long time to recover from exposure to bright lights – a quick flash of a torch or car headlights and a frog's vision is so compromised it can take hours for it to recover, preventing it from performing the evening's important duties of foraging, calling, mating or laying spawn.[8]

Birds are also very vulnerable to the effects of artificial light. Numerous studies reveal that almost every aspect of bird behaviour is being disrupted. Artificial light tricks birds into thinking it's spring – the dawn chorus is starting too early, both in time and season, and birds exposed to artificial light before dawn sing for too long, leaving them with less time to mate and forage. Artificial light also fools female birds into laying their eggs too early in the year and, by lighting up their nesting sites and foraging spaces, exposes them to predation.[9] Artificial light from urban centres can cause flocks to become lost, disorientated or so dazzled they collide with large buildings. From flashing lights on skyscrapers to the constant, glowing mantle above an area of urban sprawl, science is only just beginning to get to grips with how human light sources are upsetting birds' innate rhythms and sense of direction. The energy needed to fly thousands of miles, in a short time window, leaves almost no room for mistakes. Turning back or redirecting a route just isn't possible. According to the United Nations, every year light pollution kills millions upon millions of migratory birds. In North America alone, it is thought that up to one billion migrating birds perish every year from collisions with buildings.

Brightly lit evenings in winter also seem to be tricking birds into thinking that spring has arrived, with its longer days and twilights, and encourages them to migrate too soon. If flocks head off earlier than they should, birds find the weather conditions en route are often unfamiliar and more challenging than they otherwise would be. And, when our exhausted travellers finally arrive, the usual seasonal food resources are not available.

Even the oceans, which for decades were believed to be immune from artificial light, are being influenced by glare from coastal zones, shipping and offshore industry. One study, for example, showed that working lights from ships in the Arctic disrupt the behaviour of fish and zooplankton that live at least 200 metres deep – the threshold of the twilight zone.[10] Other studies suggest that light from vessels and other manmade ocean structures is discouraging the twilight zone's creatures, who migrate under the cover of dusk and pull the world's carbon dioxide out of harm's way, from coming up to the surface at all.[11]

There are few places, it seems, immune from our insistence on turning dusk, night and dawn into permanent daylight. The invention of electric lighting, and its pervasive reach into nearly every corner of modern life, has radically altered the natural rhythms that once governed our existence. But as we bask in the glow of artificial light, it's worth asking: what toll is this obsession taking on our health and well-being? As French geologist Michel Siffre so punishingly demonstrated in his self-imposed isolation in total darkness for several months, the absence of natural light can have devastating consequences on our body's internal clock and our mental wellbeing. While few of us will ever experience complete darkness for months on end, the ways in which artificial light reshapes our environment – and, by extension, our biology – are profound and far-reaching.

If experiencing dusk and dawn are so important for our natural rhythms, what happens if we don't? The answer is that we don't really know. Or, at least, we are only just beginning to understand how interlinked and nuanced these effects are. We've long known that our circadian rhythms control almost everything we do. Our sleep-wake cycle, body temperature, energy levels, digestion, metabolism, appetite, hormones and many other physiological functions can become compromised if our internal clock has lost its tempo. From obesity to diabetes, sleep disorders to depression, many of the world's most intractable and chronic health problems have been linked to out-of-sync circadian rhythms. Night-shift workers, for example, are 10 per cent more likely to die earlier than their day-working colleagues.[12] Similar research showed the brains of workers who'd done ten years of night shifts prematurely aged by nearly seven years.[13] It was once thought that, after a relatively short period, most people's bodies could adapt well to working at night. Current studies suggest that they don't. Ever.

In our modern, constantly lit lives, our circadian rhythms still hold us to a routine that evolved tens or even hundreds of thousands of years ago. And yet, these rhythms are deep within us, even at a genetic level. When the ancestors of modern humans migrated out of Africa into the Middle East, Europe and beyond around 70,000 years ago, they had to contend with seasons and day lengths different to those from the climate they had evolved in. Already living in these more northerly latitudes, however, were Neanderthals and other archaic hominids who had left Africa hundreds of thousands of years before and had had time to adapt. Geneticists now believe that our ability to cope with seasonal variations in daylight or 'photoperiod' is a trait we inherited from our Neanderthal cousins through interbreeding.[14] In fact, all non-African modern humans are thought to carry between 1 and 4 per cent Neanderthal DNA, bits of genetic code that tweaked our circadian rhythms forever.

Unbreakable ties to our circadian rhythm, and our deep relationship with twilight, can also be seen in patterns of childbirth. A study involving various London universities and the National Childbirth Trust (NCT) looked at the timings of over five million human births over the period between 2005 and 2014. Spontaneous births – those that happened without Caesarean or induction – showed an incredibly consistent pattern. Over half of all the babies born arrived between 1 a.m. and 7 a.m., with a noticeable peak around 4 a.m. This trend, to give birth in the early hours of the morning, is almost certainly a relic of our evolutionary heritage. Giving birth is a vulnerable time; childbirth in the daylight may seem like a good idea but it may have been safer to wait until morning's twilight, when your tribe were gathered closely together as a protective unit. It may have also made sense to wait until dawn, when fellow group members would be emerging from sleep and more alert than earlier in the evening, ready to swing into action if danger arose.[15] Of my three daughters, two were born at morning's twilight. The third only arrived out of this sequence because I was induced four weeks early, an experience that my wracked body fought against from start to finish.

One of the most important biological processes tied to twilight is the production of melatonin, a hormone crucial to regulating sleep and wake cycles. Melatonin levels are low during the day and begin to rise with the onset of dusk, peaking in the middle of the night before tapering off at dawn. This natural cycle allows us to fall asleep at night and wake up feeling refreshed in the morning. The introduction of electric lighting has profoundly altered this process. In our modern, artificially illuminated world, we spend much of our time indoors, often under dim or low-quality lighting. Additionally, the widespread use of mobile phones, computers and television screens - which give out blue light - has been shown to delay the onset of melatonin production, making it harder for us to fall asleep. Research at the University of Colorado demonstrated the impact of artificial lighting on melatonin rhythms. When participants spent a week camping in the Rocky Mountains, exposed only to natural sunlight and campfire light, their circadian rhythms realigned with the natural day-night cycle. Melatonin production occurred earlier, and their sleep-wake cycles became more synchronised with the natural world.[16]

But does it really matter if our body clocks are matched to natural light in this way? The answer is that if you are exposed to artificial light late into the evening, not only is your brain aroused but the delayed onset of melatonin production can make it difficult to get to sleep. In the morning, by contrast, the fact that your body is still producing melatonin means that it is more difficult to wake up and you feel less alert in the first few hours of being up and about. This is called 'phase delay' and has been linked to sleep disorders such as insomnia, as well as other health issues like mood disturbances, depression and anxiety. Disruption of your circadian rhythm can also lead to poor metabolic health, including increased risk for obesity, diabetes and cardiovascular disease; it can inhibit immune system function too.

To mitigate this, many devices and screens now have blue light filters, or you can use apps that reduce blue light exposure in the evening and better mimic the changes in both colour and intensity of light that happen through the day. This is not a book about biophilic design. But it is cheering that interest in biodynamic lighting - indoor illumination that mimics the natural patterns of the day - is also growing. Our understanding of how the human body responds to natural light is constantly evolving. With this knowledge comes new technology. There are now lamps, for example, that change colour temperature and intensity based on the patterns of daylight at your exact location. They also adjust automatically through the year as day lengths change.

There's also been some interesting research into the effect of simulated twilight on people with disrupted circadian rhythms. Patients with Seasonal Affective Disorder, for example, have been shown to benefit from being exposed to simulated dawn in their bedrooms in the final period of sleep. This slow ramping up in the intensity and colour of natural light seems to not only have an antidepressant effect but also resets the body clock: patients stop producing melatonin at the correct time and this helps them feel alert on waking. Dementia patients are particularly prone to disrupted circadian rhythms. The disease can directly affect the brain's circadian patterns but many people who experience neurodegenerative issues also have reduced access to natural light, often due to institutionalisation and lack of time outdoors. Sleep problems and evening agitation, a behaviour called 'sundowning', are very common as a result and distressing. A brilliant piece of recent Swiss research, however, introduced simulated twilight lighting to patients' rooms. The light source replicated both the intensity and spectral range of dusk and dawn over a period of seventeen weeks and, in a result that should inform institutional lighting design around the world, patients reported feeling more cheerful and uplifted, especially on waking up, and experienced much less fragmented sleep.[17]

I think we are all starting to grasp that something is amiss. A quick trawl of social media reveals a host of health trends related to light and well-being: from blue-light-filtering spectacles to relax you in the evening, to 'twilight beauty' routines, designed to help people disconnect from their working day. While it would be easy to dismiss such quick fixes as quackery, their presence and popularity shows how desperate people are for a solution. For most of us, however, perhaps the most important thing to take from this book is just how important it is to spend time outdoors, in natural light.

And, if possible, to seek out opportunities to experience dawn and dusk at different times of the year.

It's also vital that we preserve and protect our intimate and ancient relationship with the sky. Many now view light pollution as an issue as serious as air or water quality. When so many living organisms, including ourselves, are being harmed, it is imperative for both governments and individuals to act. Thankfully, many different organisations - from Dark Skies International (who advocate for protecting the night sky) to Light Aware (who focus on the effects of lighting on human health) - are campaigning to raise awareness and make policy changes that positively impact both communities and wildlife. There is also a greater understanding of how to tackle some of its more pernicious effects without compromising safety or practicality.

On an individual level, we can do plenty. Dark sky experts recommend only lighting what you need, when you need to - in other words, every light source needs a purpose. In practical terms, this means things like reducing both the intensity and quantity of garden and security lighting, using timer or motion controls, turning off lights when not in use, shielding light sources so they don't point upwards towards the sky, and sticking to warmer colour temperatures for outdoor lights that closer mimic the end of the day (most research suggests that low-intensity lighting and warmer hues such as warm white, yellow or amber are less confusing for insects). Twilight is even inspiring some of the solutions. Researchers are looking at the specific gene that allows bioluminescent life to glow and using it to create light-emitting plants to illuminate our homes, offices and other public spaces in a more sustainable way. MIT engineers, for example, tweaked watercress to create a plant that gave off gentle light for nearly four hours,[18] an interesting project that its researchers hope may eventually lead to self-powered, wildlife-friendly light sources.

Life on the smallholding puts me in direct contact with both wildlife and domesticated animals, weather and light. I am outdoors, a lot. Just living here, and having to engage with every aspect of growing food and caring for animals, my profound love for the natural world has deepened with every day that passes. That familiarity and respect has brought me to a point when I'm not only astonished by the breathtaking complexity and brilliance of nature, but I am really struck by how little we understand of it. We all look at the natural world through a uniquely narrow lens and can hardly imagine that other living things - whether they're plants or creatures, on land or in the sea - have any other way of interacting with our planet than we do. And yet, twilight has shown me that there are multiple worlds on ours, ones inhabited by life that uses different senses or senses different things. It's truly humbling and we don't even know what we don't know. Spending time in twilight and *really* noticing it, especially over the past year, I feel I have reconnected with something that previous generations knew in their bones; that these two liminal periods of the day are important and powerful. I'm also dazzled, in every sense, by the modern world and find myself increasingly irritated with our insistence on shining a bright, artificial light on everything we do. Much more interesting things are happening in the half-light.

Twilight is the blazing cauldron that separates day from night. And, like many things in life, we have lost touch with its magic. For thousands of years we paid attention to twilight, lost ourselves in its colours, moods and strange happenings. It also helped us understand our place in the scheme of things. These special times of day used to matter and yet, over a very short period of time in human terms, we have flicked off our interest like a switch. Perhaps it's time we let twilight beguile us again.

When I am dead, my dearest,
Sing no sad songs for me;

THE SECRET WORLD OF TWILIGHT

Plant thou no roses at my head,
Nor shady cypress tree:
Be the green grass above me
With showers and dewdrops wet;
And if thou wilt, remember,
And if thou wilt, forget.

I shall not see the shadows,
I shall not feel the rain;
I shall not hear the nightingale
Sing on, as if in pain:
And dreaming through the twilight
That doth not rise nor set,
Haply I may remember,
And haply may forget.

'When I am dead, my dearest' by Christina Rossetti
(1848)

Notes

Chapter 1

1. Goldstein, B. R., *Theory and observation in ancient and medieval astronomy* (London: Variorum Reprints, 1985), p. 110.
2. Beech, M., 'Atmospheric Height by Twilight's Glow', *Journal of the Royal Astronomical Society of Canada*, Vol. 104, No. 4 (Aug. 2010), p. 147.
3. Plair, P., 'There Are Three Types of Twilight', *Scientific American* (a Division of Springer Nature America, Inc., 1 Nov. 2024).
4. *The Standard* (30 Nov. 1883), p. 5.
5. *Nature* (3 Jan. 1884), p. 222, www.nature.com/articles/029222a0.pdf
6. Ibid.
7. Hamblyn, R., 'The Krakatoa Sunsets', *The Public Domain Review*, https://publicdomainreview.org/essay/the-krakatoa-sunsets/
8. Ascroft, W., *Catalogue of Sky Sketches from September 1883 to September 1886* (United Kingdom: Science Museum, 1888), p. 2.
9. Jones, J., 'How The Scream became the ultimate image for our political age', *The Guardian* (16 Jan. 2019), www.theguardian.com/artanddesign/2019/jan/16/the-scream-edvard-munch-ultimate-image-political-age-british-museum

10 Howe, S., in *Backpacker Magazine* (Active Interest Media, Inc., April 1996), p. 62.
11 Wallis, F., *Bede: The Reckoning of Time* (Liverpool University Press, 1999), pp. lxvii-lxviii.
12 Chisholm, G. G., *The World As It Is: A Popular Account of the Countries and Peoples of the Earth* (United Kingdom: Blackie, 1884), p. xix.
13 Dickens, C., *The Haunted Man and the Ghost's Bargain* (London: Chapman & Hall, 1899), pp. 5-6.
14 Cornelius Tacitus, 'The Life of Cnaeus Julius Agricola' in *The Complete Works of Tacitus 677* (Moses Hadas ed., Alfred John Church & William Jackson Brodribb trans., 1942), chpt. 12.3.
15 Goodlad, L., 'Why Shetlanders love "da simmer dim"', www.shetland.org/blog/shetland-simmer-dim

Twilight Diary – Winter

1 'Towards the Break of Day' in Yeats, W. B., Finneran, R. J., *The Collected Poems of W. B. Yeats* (United Kingdom: Scribner, 1996), p. 185.
2 Ibid., p. 789.
3 Edmondston, T., *An Etymological Glossary of the Shetland and Orkney Dialect* (Edinburgh: Adam and Charles Black, 1866), www.google.co.uk/books/edition/An_Etymological_Glossary_of_the_Shetland/GHmuYm4_TgwC?hl=en&gbpv=1&dq=dagset&pg=PA23&printsec=frontcover
4 Jacob, G., *The Modern Justice: Containing the Business of a Justice of Peace, in All Its Parts* (United Kingdom: assignee of Edward Sayer, Esq, 1716), p. 316.
5 Hay, D., 'Working Time, Dinner Time, Serving Time: Labour and Law in Industrialisation', *University of Oxford Discussion Papers in Economic and Social History*, No. 164 (May 2018), p. 4.

6   Ross, F. et al., *A Glossary of Words Used in Holderness in the East-riding of Yorkshire* (United Kingdom: Trübner, 1877), p. 5.
7   Forrester, J., *Dialogues on the passions, habits, and affections peculiar to children* (London, 1748), p. 40, https://wellcomecollection.org/works/xjdxzv6k/items
8   Willard, H. M., 'Children's Fears' in *The Journal of Education* (United States: Boston University, School of Education, 1894), pp. 163-4, www.google.co.uk/books/edition/The_Journal_of_Education/-axPAQAAMAAJ?hl=en&gbpv=1&dq=teaching+children+not+to+fear+the+dark&pg=PA164&printsec=frontcover
9   Robson, G., *Home Study: An Elementary Journal for Students of Mechanics, Electricity, Etc.* (United States: Colliery Engineer Company, 1898), p. 63.
10 Swift, J., *Directions to Servants in General: And in Particular the Butler, Cook, Footman, Coachman, Groom, House-steward, and Land-steward, Porter, Dairy-maid, Chamber-maid, Nurse, Laundress, House-keeper, Tutoress, Or Governess* (United Kingdom: R. Dodsley and M. Cooper, 1745), p. 25.
11 Gaskell, E. C., 'Chapter V. Old Letters', *Cranford* (London: J. M. Dent & Co, New York: E. P. Dutton & Co, 1904), www.gutenberg.org/ebooks/394
12 Garnert, J., 'Anden i lampan. Etnologiska perspektivpa ljus och morker' (Stockholm: Carlsson, 1993), quoted in Löfgren, O., and Ehn, B., 'Daydreaming Between Dusk and Dawn', *Etnofoor*, 20(2) (2007), p. 11, www.jstor.org/stable/25758137
13 Garnert, J. (trans. Jonathon Mair), 'On the cultural history of Nordic light and lighting', p. 10, www.jangarnert.se/bilder/Jan%20Garnert%20essay.pdf
14 Columella, *De Re Rustica*, 7.12.43., www.thelatinlibrary.com/columella/columella.rr7.shtml

Chapter 2

1. Sturm, C. C., *Reflections on the works of God, and of His providence, throughout all nature, for every day in the year,* Translated first from the German of Mr. C. C. Sturm. By a lady. Fourth edition (Ireland: William Jones, 1792), p. 231, www.google.co.uk/books/edition/Reflections_on_the_works_of_God_and_of_H/xT9N2CqrUdkC?hl=en&gbpv=0
2. Fleissner, G., Fleissner, G., 'Perception of Natural Zeitgeber Signals', in Kumar, V. (ed.), *Biological Rhythms* (Springer, Berlin, Heidelberg, 2002), https://doi.org/10.1007/978-3-662-06085-8_8
3. Woelders, T., Wams, E., Gordijn, M., Beersma, D. and Hut, R., *Integration of color and intensity increases time signal stability for the human circadian system when sunlight is obscured by clouds,* Scientific Reports (2018), 8. 10.1038/s41598-018-33606-5.
4. Siffre, M., '30th August 1962' in *Beyond Time* (United Kingdom: McGraw-Hill, 1964).
5. www.newscientist.com/article/mg23931900-400-this-man-spent-months-alone-underground-and-it-warped-his-mind/
6. Benoit, J., 'Le rôle des yeux dans l'action stimulante de la lumière sur le développement testiculaire chez le canard', *C R Seances Soc Biol Fil* (1935), 118: 669–671.
7. Fosbury, R. A. E. and Glen, J., 'Reindeer eyes seasonally adapt to ozone-blue Arctic twilight by tuning a photonic tapetum lucidum', *Proc. R. Soc.* (2022), B.28920221002, http://doi.org/10.1098/rspb.2022.1002
8. Zaidi, F. H., *et al.*, 'Short-Wavelength Light Sensitivity of Circadian, Pupillary, and Visual Awareness in Humans Lacking an Outer Retina', *Current Biology,* Vol. 17, Issue 24, pp. 2122-2128.

9 Sun L., Peräkylä J., Kovalainen A., Ogawa K. H., Karhunen P. J. and Hartikainen K. M., 'Human Brain Reacts to Transcranial Extraocular Light', *PLoS One* (24 Feb. 2016), https://www.researchgate.net/publication/295858378 _Human_Brain_Reacts_to_Transcranial_Extraocular_Light
10 Cordani, L., Tagliazucchi, E., Vetter, C., *et al.*, 'Endogenous modulation of human visual cortex activity improves perception at twilight', *Nat Commun* 9, 1274 (2018), https://doi.org/10.1038/s41467-018-03660-8
11 Herz, R. S., *et al.*, 'The Influence of Circadian Timing on Olfactory Sensitivity', *Chemical Senses*, Vol. 43, Issue 1 (Jan. 2018), pp. 45-51, https://doi.org/10.1093/chemse/bjx067
12 Kwon, Y. H., Nam, K. S., 'Circadian fluctuations in three types of sensory modules in healthy subjects', *Neural Regen Res.* (15 Feb. 2014), https://pubmed.ncbi.nlm.nih.gov/25206832/
13 Mooney, J., 'Diurnal variation of threshold skin sensation', Doctoral thesis (Ph.D), UCL (University College London, 1999), https://discovery.ucl.ac.uk/id/eprint/10103508/
14 Miller, M. W. and Gronfier, C., 'Diurnal variation of the startle reflex in relation to HPA-axis activity in humans', *Psychophysiology* (May 2006), https://pubmed.ncbi.nlm.nih.gov/16805869/
15 Koizumi, T., Suzuki, T., Pillai, N. S., Bies, R. R., Takeuchi, H., Yoshimura, K., Mimura, M. and Uchida, H., 'Circadian patterns of hallucinatory experiences in patients with schizophrenia: Potentials for chrono-pharmacology', *J Psychiatr Res.* (Oct. 2019), https://pubmed.ncbi.nlm.nih.gov/31254838/
16 Dryden, J. and Lee, N., *Oedipus: A Tragedy* (London, 1679), p. 50.

17 Dickens, C., *The Haunted Man and the Ghost's Bargain* (London: Chapman & Hall, 1899), pp.7-8.
18 Jones, T. W., 'The Wisdom and Beneficence of the Almighty, as Displayed in the Sense of Vision', The Actonian Prize Essay for 1851 (United Kingdom, 1851), p. 86.
19 *Rauðúlfs þáttr*, as translated by Vilhjalmsson, T., 'Time and Travel in Old Norse Society', *Disputatio*. 2 (2023).
20 Le Floch, A., *et al.*, 'The sixteenth century Alderney crystal: a calcite as an efficient reference optical compass?' (2013), *Proc. R. Soc. A*.469 20120651, https://royalsocietypublishing.org/doi/10.1098/rspa.2012.0651

Twilight Diary – Spring

1 Wong, M. K. L. and Didham, R. K., 'Global meta-analysis reveals overall higher nocturnal than diurnal activity in insect communities', *Nat Commun* 15, 3236 (2024), https://doi.org/10.1038/s41467-024-47645-2
2 Thompson, M. L., 'Some Notes on the Long-Eared Bat in Captivity', *The Naturalist* (Simpkin, Marshall, 1892), p. 18.
3 *The Gentleman's Magazine* (United Kingdom: n.p., 1732), p. 907.
4 Ovid, *Metamorphoses*, Book IV (trans. A. S. Kline), Bk IV:389-415, 'The daughters of Minyas become bats', https://ovid.lib.virginia.edu/trans/Metamorph4.htm#478205199
5 Harris, T. M., *The natural history of the Bible ; or, A description of all the quadrupeds, birds, fishes, reptiles, and insects, trees, plants, flowers, gums, and precious stones, mentioned in the sacred scriptures: Collected from the best authorities, and alphabetically arranged* (London: T. Tegg, 1824).
6 Seager, H. W., *Natural History in Shakespeare's Time: Being Extracts Illustrative of the Subject as He Knew it* (United Kingdom: E. Stock, 1896), p. 27, www.google.co.uk

/books/edition/Natural_History_in_Shakespeare_s_Time
/EzZaAAAAMAAJ?hl=en&gbpv=1&dq=read+books+in+a
+dark+night,+anoint+your+face+with+the+blood+of+a
+Bat'&pg=PA27&printsec=frontcover

7 Riccucci, M., 'Bats as materia medica: an ethnomedical review and implications for conservation', *Vespertilio* (2013), 16. pp. 249-270.

8 Alighieri, D., *Dante's Inferno* (trans. Rev. Henry Francis Carey), (New York : Cassell, Petter, Galpin & Co., 1866), p. 181.

9 Stoker, B., *Dracula*, 'Chapter XII Dr. Seward's Diary. 20 September' (New York: Grosset & Dunlap, 1897), https://gutenberg.org/cache/epub/345/pg345-images.html

10 Cranbrook, 'Notes & Observations' in Volume 11 (1959–1961) Part 2 (1959), p. 193, and Part 3 (1960), p. 271, *Transactions of the Suffolk Naturalists' Society*, www.suffolkbis.org.uk/publications/tsns/11

11 Kirk, R., *The Secret Commonwealth or A Treatise displayeing the Chiefe Curiosities as they are in Use among diverse of the People of Scotland to this Day; SINGULARITIES for the most Part peculiar to that Nation (1691)*, reprinted in Lang, A., *The Secret Commonwealth of Elves, Fauns and Fairies* (Stirling, Scotland: The Observer Press, 1933), p. 67, https://openbooks.is.ed.ac.uk/record/97439/1/0006806c.pdf

12 Thompson, M. P., 'In the Jura', *The Catholic World: A Monthly Magazine of General Literature and Science* (United States: Paulist Fathers, Sept. 1886), p. 774.

13 *The Gentleman's Magazine* (United Kingdom: Bradbury, Evans, 1881), p. 345.

14 Arbit, J., 'Diurnal cycles and learning in earthworms', *Science* (1957); 126(3275):654-655. doi:10.1126/science.126.3275.654-a

15 *Hand-book about our domestic pets* (United Kingdom: Cassell, Petter & Galpin, n.p., 1862), p. 63.
16 Sackville-West, V., *V. Sackville-West's Garden book: A collection taken from In your garden, In your garden again, More for your garden, Even more for your garden* (London: Michael Joseph, 1968), p. 126.
17 Ibid., p. 69.

Chapter 3

1 Gerard, J., *The Herball, or Generall History of Plants*, chpt. 58, 'Of the Marvel of Peru', www.exclassics.com/herbal/herbalv20059.htm
2 Jette T. K, *et al.*, 'Trends in floral scent chemistry in pollination syndromes: floral scent composition in moth-pollinated taxa', *Botanical Journal of the Linnean Society*, Vol. 113, Issue 3 (Nov. 1993), pp. 263-284, https://doi.org/10.1111/j.1095-8339.1993.tb00340.x
3 Raguso, R. A., Levin, R. A., Foose, S. E., Holmberg, M. W. and McDade, L. A., 'Fragrance chemistry, nocturnal rhythms and pollination "syndromes"', *Nicotiana. Phytochemistry* (2003), 63, pp. 265-284.
4 BBC News, 'Stinky bloom of "corpse flower" enthrals thousands' (22 Jan. 2025), www.bbc.co.uk/news/articles/cvgpnqe91j10
5 Porter, D. and Graham, P., *Darwin's Sciences* (United Kingdom: Wiley, 2016), p. 103.
6 Fenske, M. P., Hewett Hazelton, K. D., Hempton, A. K., *et al.*, 'Circadian clock gene LATE ELONGATED HYPOCOTYL directly regulates the timing of floral scent emission in Petunia', *Proc Natl Acad Sci U S A* (2015); 112(31):9775-9780. doi:10.1073/pnas.1422875112.

7 www.theweatherprediction.com/wx&timeofday/
8 Cooley, J., 'Floral Heat Rewards and Direct Benefits to Insect Pollinators', *Annals of the Entomological Society of America* (1995), 88. pp. 576-579. www.researchgate.net/publication/233507467_Floral_Heat_Rewards_and_Direct_Benefits_to_Insect_Pollinators
9 Knop, E., Gerpe, C., Ryser, R., Hofmann, F., Menz, M. H. M., Trösch, S., Ursenbacher, S., Zoller, L. and Fontaine, C., 'Rush hours in flower visitors over a day-night cycle', *Insect Conservation and Diversity* (2018), 11(3), 267-275, https://doi.org/10.1111/icad.12277
10 Macgregor, C. J. and Scott-Brown, A. S., 'Nocturnal pollination: an overlooked ecosystem service vulnerable to environmental change', *Emerg Top Life Sci* (2 Jul. 2020); https://pubmed.ncbi.nlm.nih.gov/32478390/
11 Pattemore, D. E., Buxton, M. N., Cutting, B. T., McBrydie, H. M., Goodwin, R. M. and Dag, A., 'Low overnight temperatures delay "Hass" avocado (*Persea americana*) female flower opening, leading to nocturnal flowering', *Journal of Pollination Ecology* (2018), 23, pp. 127-135, https://doi.org/10.26786/1920-7603(2018)12
12 Walton R. E., *et al.*, 'Nocturnal pollinators strongly contribute to pollen transport of wildflowers in an agricultural landscape', *Biol. Lett.* (16 May 2020), 20190877, https://doi.org/10.1098/rsbl.2019.0877
13 Robertson, S. M., Dowling, A. P. G., Wiedenmann, R. N., Joshi, N. K. and Westerman, E. L., 'Nocturnal Pollinators Significantly Contribute to Apple Production', *Journal of Economic Entomology*, Vol. 114, Issue 5 (Oct. 2021), pp. 2155-2161, https://doi.org/10.1093/jee/toab145

14 Ellis, E. E., Edmondson, J. L., Maher, K. H., Hipperson, H. and Campbell, S. A., 'Negative effects of urbanisation on diurnal and nocturnal pollen-transport networks', *Ecology Letters* (2023), 26, pp. 1382-1393, https://doi.org/10.1111/ele.14261

15 Gerard, J., *The Herbal, or General History of Plants*, chpt. 253, 'Of Goat's-Beard, or Go-To-Bed-At-Noon', www.exclassics.com/herbal/herbalv30079.htm

16 Calhoun, T. L. & Potter, J. M. (eds) *Andrew Marvel The Garden* (Columbus, Ohio: Merrill 1970) pp49-50 https://archive.org/details/gardenoooomarv

17 Kagan, I. A., et al., 'Seasonal and Diurnal Variation in Water-Soluble Carbohydrate Concentrations of Repeatedly Defoliated Red and White Clovers in Central Kentucky', *Journal of Equine Veterinary Science*, Vol. 84, 2020, 102858, https://doi.org/10.1016/j.jevs.2019.102858, www.sciencedirect.com/science/article/pii/S0737080619306070

18 Mehta, D., Scandola, S., Kennedy, C., Lummer C., Gallo, M. C. R., Grubb, L. E., Tan, M., Scarpella, E. and Uhrig, R. G., 'Twilight length alters growth and flowering time in Arabidopsis via *LHY/CCA1*', *Sci Adv.* (28 Jun. 2024); https://pubmed.ncbi.nlm.nih.gov/38941453/

Twilight Diary – Spring/Summer

1 https://bosworthtoller.com/search?q=uht

2 Cheng, M. F., 'For whom does the female dove coo? A case for the role of vocal self-stimulation', *Animal Behaviour* (1992), Vol. 43, Issue 6, pp. 1035-1044, https://doi.org/10.1016/S0003-3472(06)80016-3.

3 Dinh, J. P., Peters, S. and Nowicki, S., 'Song performance improves with continued singing across the morning in

a songbird', *Animal Behaviour* (2020), Vol. 167, pp. 127-137, https://doi.org/10.1016/j.anbehav.2020.06.018.

Chapter 4

1. Pliny the Elder, *Natural History*, Book 10, XXIV-XXV, https://bestiary.ca/beasts/beastsource258.htm
2. Hymns of Prudentius, 'Hymn at Cock-Crow', https://ccel.org/ccel/prudentius/cathimerinon/cathimerinon.p01t.html
3. Carr, W., *The Dialect of Craven: In the West-Riding of the County of York* (United Kingdom: W. Crofts, 1828), p. 152.
4. Bechstein, J. M. and Adams, H. G., *Cage and Chamber-birds: Their Natural History, Habits, Food, Diseases, Management, and Modes of Capture* (United Kingdom: H. G. Bohn, 1856), p. 28.
5. *The Child's Friend* (London: George Lamb, 1872), Vol. VIII, p. 11.
6. Cooper, N. W., Dossman, B. C., Berrigan, L. E., et al., 'Songbirds initiate migratory flights synchronously relative to civil dusk', *Mov Ecol* 11, 24 (2023), https://doi.org/10.1186/s40462-023-00382-5
7. Dokter, A. M., et al., 'Twilight ascents by Common Swifts, *Apus apus*, at dawn and dusk: acquisition of orientation cues?', *Animal Behaviour* (2013), 85(3): pp. 545-552.
8. Burton, J. and Taylor, K., *Nightwatch: The Natural World from Dusk to Dawn* (London: Michael Joseph, 1983), p. 15.
9. L. M. San-Jose, et al., 'Differential fitness effects of moonlight on plumage colour morphs in barn owls', *Nature, Ecology & Evolution* (2019), 3, pp. 1331-40, https://doi.org/10.1038/s41559-019-0967-2

10 Waterton, C., 'Letter to Lady Cullum, regarding: his approach to natural history, shipwreck, indisposition, temperance campaigner Father Mathew in Wakefield, lions and lion cubs, "little roman owls"' (12 Jul. 1842), www.richardfordmanuscripts.co.uk/catalogue/22376

11 *The Naturalist* (United Kingdom: Simpkin, Marshall, 1897), p. 76.

Twilight Diary – Summer

1 Arkle, J., 'Dragonflies in 1897', *The Entomologist* (United Kingdom: Simpkin, Marshall & Company, 1898), p. 34.

2 *The Philosophical magazine and journal: comprehending the various branches of science, the liberal and fine arts, geology, agriculture, manufactures and commerce* (United Kingdom: Cadell & Davies, 1824), p. 90.

3 *Encyclopædia Britannica: Or, A Dictionary of Arts and Science, Compiled Upon a New Plan* (United Kingdom: A. Bell, 1810), p. 69.

4 Nummert, G., Ritson, K. and Nemvalts, K., 'Photoluminescence in the Garden dormouse (*Eliomys quercinus*)', *Zoology*, Vol. 157, 2023, 126075, ISSN 0944-2006.

5 Hamchand R., Lafountain, A. M., Büchel R., Maas, K. R., Hird, S. M., Warren, M., Frank, H. A. and Brückner, C., 'Red Fluorescence of European Hedgehog (*Erinaceus europaeus*) Spines Results from Free-Base Porphyrins of Potential Microbial Origin', *J Chem Ecol.* (Jun. 2021); 47(6): pp. 588-596. https://pubmed.ncbi.nlm.nih.gov/33948884/

6 www.scientificamerican.com/article/transgenic-tadpole-glows-to-reveal-chemical-contamination/

Chapter 5

1. www.sciencefocus.com/nature/scientists-have-discovered-a-pigbutt-worm-whose-farts-glow-green
2. Thomas, K. N., Robison, B. H. and Johnsen, S., 'Two eyes for two purposes: In situ evidence for asymmetric vision in the cockeyed squids *Histioteuthis heteropsis* and *Stigmatoteuthis dofleini*', *Philosophical Transactions of the Royal Society B* (2017), https://royalsocietypublishing.org/doi/10.1098/rstb.2016.0069
3. Irigoien, X., Klevjer, T., Røstad, A., *et al.*, 'Large mesopelagic fishes biomass and trophic efficiency in the open ocean', *Nat Commun* 5, 3271 (2014), https://doi.org/10.1038/ncomms4271
4. Cohen, J. H., Last, K. S., Charpentier, C. L., Cottier, F., Daase, M., Hobbs, L., Johnsen, G. and Berge, J., 'Photophysiological cycles in Arctic krill are entrained by weak midday twilight during the Polar Night', *PLOS Biology* (2021); 19 (10): https://pubmed.ncbi.nlm.nih.gov/34665816/

Twilight Diary – Autumn

1. C. Julius Caesar, *Gallic War*, trans. McDevitte, W. A., Bohn, W. S. (first edition, New York: Harper & Brothers, Harper's New Classical Library, 1869), Book 6, chpt. 18, http://data.perseus.org/texts/urn:cts:latinLit:phi0448.phi001.perseus-eng1
2. 'Seven-stone Antas, Portugal/Spain (multiple locations): General Description', *The Portal to the Heritage of Astronomy* (UNESCO International Working Group on Astronomy and World Heritage), https://web.astronomicalheritage.net/show-entity?identity=50&idsubentity=1

3 'Chankillo Archaeoastronomical Complex', *The Portal to the Heritage of Astronomy* (UNESCO International Working Group on Astronomy and World Heritage), https://whc.unesco.org/en/list/1624/
4 Silva, F. and Campion, N., *Skyscapes: The Role and Importance of the Sky in Archaeology* (Illustrated edition, Oxbow Books, 2015).
5 Hayden, B. and Villeneuve, S., 'Astronomy in the Upper Palaeolithic?', *Cambridge Archaeological Journal* (McDonald Institute for Archaeological Research, 2011), 21:3, pp. 331-55. doi:10.1017/S0959774311000400, www.cambridge.org/core/services/aop-cambridge-core/content/view/DF41D037273839A3793C15CCEF250AB8/S0959774311000400a.pdf/astronomy_in_the_upper_palaeolithic.pdf
6 Ronnberg, A. (ed.), *The Book of Symbols: 'Reflections on Archetypal Images'* (TASCHEN, Illustrated edition, 2022), p. 88.
7 *The Dublin University Magazine* (1871), Vol. 77, p. 91.
8 *Chambers's Journal of Popular Literature, Science and Arts* (United Kingdom: W & R Chambers, 9 Mar., 1878), pp. 146-7.
9 Ibid., p. 147.
10 https://post.parliament.uk/research-briefings/post-pb-0054/

Chapter 6

1 Hölker, F., Wolter, C., Perkin, E. K. and Tockner, K., 'Light pollution as a biodiversity threat', *Trends Ecol. Evol.*, 25 (2010), pp. 681-682, 10.1016/j.tree.2010.09.007
2 Knop, E., Zoller, L., Ryser, R., *et al.*, 'Artificial light at night as a new threat to pollination', *Nature* (2017), 548, pp. 206-209, https://doi.org/10.1038/nature23288

3. Fabian, S. T., Sondhi, Y., Allen, P. E., *et al.*, 'Why flying insects gather at artificial light', *Nat Commun* 15, 689 (2024), https://doi.org/10.1038/s41467-024-44785-3
4. Cao Yu, Zhang Shuang, Ma Ke-Ming, 'Artificial light at night decreases leaf herbivory in typical urban areas Frontiers', *Plant Science* (2024) 15, www.frontiersin.org/journals/plant-science/articles/10.3389/fpls.2024.1392262
5. Kivelä, L., Elgert, C., Lehtonen, T. K. and Candolin, U., 'The color of artificial light affects mate attraction in the common glow-worm', *Science of The Total Environment*, Vol. 857, Part 3, 2023,159451,ISSN 0048-9697, https://doi.org/10.1016/j.scitotenv.2022.159451.
6. Voigt, C. C., Dekker, J., Fritze, M., Gazaryan, S., Hölker, F., Jones, G., Lewanzik, D., Limpens, H. J. G. A., Mathews, F., Rydell, J., Spoelstra, K. and Zagmajster, M., 'The Impact Of Light Pollution On Bats Varies According To Foraging Guild And Habitat Context', *BioScience* (Oct. 2021), Vol. 71, Issue 10, pp. 1103–1109, https://doi.org/10.1093/biosci/biab087
7. Mittmannsgruber, M., Kavassilas, Z., Spangl, B., *et al.*, 'Artificial light at night reduces earthworm activity but increases growth of invasive ragweed', *BMC Ecol Evo.* (2024), 24, 10, https://doi.org/10.1186/s12862-024-02200-x
8. Welch, D. M., Treviño, K., Ruggles, C. L. N., Rich, C., Longcore, T., Hearnshaw, J. B., Gyarmathy, I., Dick, R., Dalton, A. and Barentine, J. C., 'The World at Night: Preserving Natural Darkness for Heritage Conservation and Night Sky Appreciation' (Switzerland: IUCN, International Union for Conservation of Nature and Natural Resources, 2024), p. 11.
9. www.bto.org/sites/default/files/u23/downloads/pdfs/BT80_EBS_article.pdf

10 Berge, J., Geoffroy, M., Daase, M., *et al.*, 'Artificial light during the polar night disrupts Arctic fish and zooplankton behaviour down to 200 m depth', *Commun Biol.* (2020), 3, 102, https://doi.org/10.1038/s42003-020-0807-6
11 https://norwegianscitechnews.com/2018/01/shedding-light-zooplankton-dark/
12 www.bbc.co.uk/news/magazine-33638905
13 Ibid.
14 Velazquez-Arcelay, K., Colbran, L. L., McArthur, E., Brand, C. M., Rinker, D. C., Siemann, J. K., McMahon, D. G. and Capra, J. A., 'Archaic Introgression Shaped Human Circadian Traits', *Genome Biology and Evolution* (Dec. 2023), Vol. 15, Issue 12, evad203, https://doi.org/10.1093/gbe/evad203
15 Martin, P., Cortina-Borja, M., Newburn, M., Harper, G., Gibson, R., Dodwell, M., *et al.*, 'Timing of singleton births by onset of labour and mode of birth in NHS maternity units in England, 2005–2014: A study of linked birth registration, birth notification, and hospital episode data' (2018), PLoS ONE 13(6): e0198183, https://doi.org/10.1371/journal.pone.0198183
16 Wright, K. P., McHill, A. W., Birks, B. R., Griffin, B. R., Rusterholz, T. and Chinoy, E. D., 'Entrainment of the Human Circadian Clock to the Natural Light-Dark Cycle', *Current Biology* (2013), Vol. 23, Issue 16, pp. 1554–1558, ISSN 0960-9822, https://doi.org/10.1016/j.cub.2013.06.039.
17 Bromundt, V., Wirz-Justice, A., Boutellier, M., Winter, S., Haberstroh, M., Terman, M. and Münch, M., 'Effects of a dawn-dusk simulation on circadian rest-activity cycles, sleep, mood and well-being in dementia patients',

Experimental Gerontology (2019), Vol. 124, 110641, https://doi.org/10.1016/j.exger.2019.110641

18 Kwak, S-Y, Giraldo, J. P., Wong, Min Hao, Koman, V. B., Lew, T. T. S., Ell, J., Weidman, M. C., Sinclair, R. M., Landry, M. P., Tisdale, W. A. and Strano, M. S., 'A Nanobionic Light-Emitting Plant', *Nano Letters* (2017), 17 (12), pp. 7951-7961.

Acknowledgements

Holly Harley – what a joy it has been to work on our first project together. You have been unfailingly brilliant and, for the record, write the most hilarious editing notes I have ever been given. Richard Milbank, huge thanks go to you for commissioning this strange and wonderful book and being my most redoubtable advocate. Jane Graham Maw – agent, friend, mentor – hugs aplenty. And, to the rest of the team at Head of Zeus, I tip my hat – you're the best.

Index

agriculture
  crops and twilight length
    134–5
  grazing animals and dusk 134
Alderney shipwreck 80–1, 86
algae 189
  bioluminescent 196–7
amphibians 70
  and artificial light 236
  biofluorescence 188
  toads 174–5, 187, 188
  see also frogs
Ancient Greeks 18, 103
anglerfish 198–9
Anne of Green Gables
    (Montgomery) 126
ants 121, 127
Arctic Ocean 206–7
Arctic reindeer 71
Aristotle 177
artists 8–9
  painting volcanic twilights
    22–4
Ascroft, William 22
Astraeus, god of dusk 221–2
astronauts 67
astronomical twilight 31–3, 33–4, 35
  and pond life 180
astronomy 15–20
  horizon astronomy 218

atmosphere
  Earth 17–19, 20, 59
  Moon 5, 59
auditory hallucinations 76
autumn 209–28

backswimmers 179, 180
Bacon, Francis 93
badgers 178
bantam cockerels 137
bar-tailed godwit 164
Barker, Cicely Mary
  Flower Fairies 101
barn owls 6, 149–53, 169–71
  plumage 170
  and rain 150–1, 152
barn swallows 181
barnacle geese 177
barrel-eye fish 200
Bartholomew the Englishman 95
bats 6, 87–90, 91–100
  and artificial light 235
  brown long-eared 89, 91–3
  daubenton's 88, 89, 97, 182
  echolocation 98, 99
  eyesight 99
  folk names for 95
  in folklore 96–8
  horseshoe 89, 98
  long-eared 97
  and moths 90–1, 98

INDEX

bats (cont'd)
  natterer's 97
  noctule 89, 97
  pipistrelle 88, 89, 90, 97
  pollinating 121, 123, 129
  scents 99–100
  South American sac-winged 99–100
  as a supposed medical remedy 94–5
  and twilight 98–9
beans 100–1
Bede, Venerable 27–9
Beech, Dr Martin 19
bees 121, 129, 177
  Central American sweat bee 126–7
beetles 90, 104, 121, 171
  carrion beetles 123
  and light pollution 233
  and polarised light 83, 84
  pollination 129
  in ponds 179
  see also fireflies; glow-worms
Benoit, Jacques 70
the Bible 93
Biddle, Violet Purton 108
big cats 61
biofluorescence 188–9
bioluminescence
  and artificial light 235
  burglar alarm bioluminescence 196–7
  counter-illumination 200–1
  fireflies 104–5, 106, 187
  glow-worms 104, 105–6, 187
  and light-emitting plants 246
  ocean creatures 196–203, 206
birds 142–53
  and artificial light 236–8
  bar-tailed godwit 164
  barn owls 6, 149–53, 169–71

barn swallows 181
  and bats 99
birdsong at dusk 148
caged birds 161–2, 164–5
crows 173, 187
dawn chorus 4, 144–8, 236
egrets 186, 187
evening pollinators 121
gulls 187
herons 185–6, 187, 189–90
hobby falcons 185
house sparrows 142–4
larks 157–8, 171–2
magpies 187
migration flights 84, 161–5, 237–8
navigation 86
nightingales 157
peregrine falcons 165–6
photoreceptors 70
  and polarised light 83, 84
poultry 136–42
quails 162–3
raptors 89
seabirds 204, 207
starlings 165–6
swifts 166–7
twilight and seasonal events 68
water-birds 178
  in winter 41
  woodland 168
blackbirds 4, 6, 144
  dawn chorus 144, 147–8
Blackhouse, James 172
blind man's holiday 51–2
blind people 71–2
blowflies 124
blue flowers 115
Blue Hour 64–5
blue light
  and circadian rhythms 242, 243
blue tits 148

INDEX

blue whales 69, 202
bluebottles 92
Britain
   seasonal variations in twilight 33–5
   UK Nautical Almanac Office 32–3
brittle stars 197
broad beans 100
Brontë, Charlotte 54
brown hawker dragonflies 182–5
brown long-eared bats 89, 91–3
Browne, William
   Britannia's Pastorals 102
Browning, Elizabeth Barrett
   'The Cat' 112–13
bugle fairy 101
būll ants 127
Burke and Hare 79
buttercups 100
butterflies 91, 121
buzzards 170

caged birds 161–2, 164–5
Canaanite mythology 222–3
carbon emissions 208, 238
carpenter ants 127
Carr, William
   The Dialect of Craven 159
caterpillars 90
cats 6, 112–14
   eyesight 114, 170
   in folklore 104
   sleeping patterns 114
cattle 134
cattle egret 186
caves, Palaeolithic 219
centipedes 109
Chambers, William 225–6
Chaucer, Geoffrey
   The Canterbury Tales 144
chickens 6, 38, 55–6, 138, 141–2, 161
chiffchaffs 144

childbirth
   and circadian rhythms 240–1
children 49–50
Christianity 158–9, 212
Chun, Carl 205
church bells 46, 47
circadian rhythms 5, 61–2, 65–9
   cockerels 160
   farm animals 140–1
   and human senses 69–80
   humans and artificial light 239–45
   and metabolic health 242–3
   and simulated twilight 243–4
civil twilight 29–31, 32–3, 34, 35
   in autumn 209
   bird migration 164
   lux levels 63
   plant research in 135
   and pond life 180, 185
   starling murmuration 166
   swifts and twilight ascent 166–7
clematis 115
climate change 135
clocks 46
clover 134
cock-eyed squid 203
cockerels 70, 136–8, 158–61
cockroaches 121
colossal squid 202
colours
   autumn skies 210, 211
   flowers at twilight 115–16
   insects and colour detection 127
   of light 24–6, 63–5
Columbus, Christopher 81
Columella, Roman farmer and writer 55
cookie-cutter shark 201
corals 61
'corpse candles' 107

INDEX

corpse flower 123
crepuscular
  meaning of the word 8
crepuscular creatures 5–7
  and vampires 96
crepuscular plants *see* plants
crepuscular pollination 121, 126–30
crickets 171, 180
crows 173

daisies 7, 100
dandelions 100
Dante
  Inferno 95–6
Dark Skies International 245
darkness, polar 35–6
Darwin, Charles 79, 132–3
Darwin, Henrietta 124
daubenton's bats 88, 89, 97, 182
Davidson, Peter
  The Idea of North 54
dawn 4, 227–8
  Anglo-Saxon word for 137
  in autumn 209–10, 211
  deities of 221, 222–3
  and folklore 102
  and human vision 73–5
  and polarised light 83–4
  swifts and twilight ascent 167
  and the three twilights 32
  vernacular names for 42–3
  winter 38–9
  and the working day 47, 48, 49
  see also sunrise
dawn chorus *see* birds
de la Mare, Walter
  'Dream Song' 43–4
deer 178
deities
  dawn and dusk 211–13
  solar and lunar 213

dementia patients 243–4
dianthus fairy 101
Dickens, Charles 9, 30–1, 77–8
diurnal organisms 5, 61
dogs 55
dormice 189
doves 146
dragonflies 182–5
Dryden, John 77
ducks 38, 56, 70, 138–40, 141
dung beetles 84
dunnocks 148
dusk 4, 5
  astronomical twilight 31–2
  autumn 210–11
  birdsong 148
  circumspection of twilight 226–7
  civil twilight 29–30
  deities of 221–3
  evening pollinators 121
  ghostly apparitions 76–9
  and human vision 73–5
  measuring time in nights 212–13
  and polarised light 83–4
  sounds of 227
  vernacular names for 41–2, 43
  Victorian appreciation of 223–5
  in winter 40–1, 51–6
  and the working day 47, 48, 49
  see also sunset

Earth
  atmosphere 17–19, 59, 63
  magnetic field 62, 84
  terminator line 59
  twilight 5, 28–9, 59–61
earthworms 109–10, 147, 148, 171, 189
  and artificial light 235–6
earwigs 90

INDEX

egrets 186, 187
Egypt, Ancient 213, 216, 222
Ehn, Billy 52-3
elves (lutins) 104
emperor hawker dragonflies 183
Eos, dawn goddess 221-2
the equator 33, 34, 35, 68
Eratosthenes, Greek astronomer 17
evening primrose 7
evening twilight *see* dusk
eyed hawkmoths 90-1
eyes
    barn owls 170
    bats and photoreceptors 99
    humans
        and ghostly apparitions 76-80
        photoreceptors 69, 71-5
    ocean twilight zone animals 201-3

fairies 101-4
falcons 185
fangtooth fish 196
Finland 54, 73
fire and light 231
fireflies 104-5, 106, 187, 196
First World War 106
fish
    anglerfish 198-9
    barrel-eye fish 200
    fangtooth fish 196
    lantern fish 205-6, 207
    marine hatchet fish 200
    photoreceptors 70
    and polarised light 83, 84
    swordfish 207
    tuna 201, 207
flies 92, 121, 129
    blowflies 124
    flesh flies 123

thunder flies 129
flowers 7
    changing colours at twilight 100, 115-16
    flower fairies 101
    fragrant 120-1, 122, 124-5, 125-6
    the 'Marvel of Peru' 119-20, 131
    and moths 90
    night-scented 90, 120-1, 124-5
    nyctinastic 130-2, 130-3
    scents 100
folklore 8
    bats 96-8
    'corpse candles' 107
    fairies 101-4
    spontaneous generation theory 177
Forbes, Edward 204-5
foxes 6, 178
French Impressionists 65
French mythology
    Dames Blanches 103-4
frogs 6, 150, 171, 174-6, 185, 186-7, 190
    and artificial light 236
fruit, pollination of 130

Garnert, Jan 53
Gaskell, Elizabeth
    Cranford 51-2
gastropods 107-9
Gathorne-Hardy, Gathorne 97-8
Gauls, Celtic tribes 212-13
geese
    barnacle geese 177
    embden goose 138-9
The Gentleman's Magazine 107
Gerard, John 119-20, 131
ghostly visions and apparitions 76-9

INDEX

the gloaming 42, 51-3, 223, 225-6
glow-worms 104, 105-7, 116, 187, 196, 235
goat's beard plant 131
Golden Hour 64
goldfinches 144, 148
Goodlad, Laurie 35
goshawks 170
Grahame, Kenneth
   Wind in the Willows 178
grasshoppers 180
greater horseshoe bats 89
Greek mythology 103
Greenhalgh, Jack 179
grey herons 185-6
Guerlain, Jacques 64-5
gulls 187

Hades, god of the underworld 195
Haidinger's brushes 85
harvestmen spiders 189
Hathor, goddess 222
Hausos, dawn goddess 221
hawker dragonflies 182-5
hawkmoths 90-1, 98, 122, 127
hearing, human sense of 76
hedgehogs 6, 110-12, 178, 189
   and artificial light 235-6
hedgerow animals 6
herbs 189
herons 185-6, 187, 189-90
Hindu festival of Chhath 222
hobby falcons 185
honeybees 121, 177
honeysuckle 7, 90, 100, 120-1
Hopkins, Gerard Manley 21-2
horizon astronomy 218
horses
   in folklore 104
   grazing 134
horseshoe bats 89, 98
house sparrows 142-4

Howe, Steve 26-7
hoya flowers 125
humans
   blind people 71-2
   circadian rhythms 69-80, 239-45
   as a diurnal and crepuscular species 61, 74-5
   effects of artificial lighting 238-47
   eyesight 69, 71-5, 115
   Neanderthal DNA in 240
   night-shift workers 239-40
   and polarised light 84-6
hunter-gatherer societies 219-20, 221

Ibn Mu'adh 15-19, 20
Icelandic spar 81-2, 85-6
Indonesian corpse flower 123
insects 7, 89, 171
   ants 121, 127
   and bats 89-90, 91
   centipedes 109
   crickets 171, 180
   earwigs 90
   flying insects and swifts 167
   and light pollution 233-4, 235
   midges 90
   millipedes 109
   mosquitoes 90
   nocturnal 90
   photoreceptors 70
   and polarised light 83, 84
   pollinators 121, 126-30
   in ponds 179-81, 182-5
   woodlice 90, 109
   see also beetles; moths
Irish folklore 104
Islam 212
   Islamic Golden Age 15-16

INDEX

jasmine 90, 100, 120-1, 122
jasmine fairy 101
Jerusalem 223
Johnson, Martin 194
Jones, Thomas Wharton 78-80
Joyce, James
  The Twilight Turns 64
Judaism 212
Julius Caesar 212-13
junglefowl 160-1

Kármán line 18-19
Kiessling, Karl Johann 23-4, 25
Kirk, Robert 102
Krakatoa twilights 20-4, 27, 95
krill, migrations of 206-7

lambs 6
lantern fish 205-6, 207
larks 157-8, 171-2
Lawrence, D.H. 9
Lee, Nathaniel 77
Lewis-Stempel, John 89
Light Aware 245
light (lux) levels 62-3
light pollution 10, 232-3, 237-8, 245-7
lighting
  artificial light 228, 231-45
  outdoor lights 245-6
  in winter 45, 48
liminal zone 8
little owls 171-3
Löfgren, Orvar 52-3
London 22, 33, 35
lupins 100
lutins (elves) 104
lux levels 62-3

Magnus, Albertus 94-5
magpies 187

Marvell, Andrew
  'The Garden' 131-2
matutinal organisms 61
melatonin 72, 241-2
metaphors 9
Mexican magnolias 127-8
Meyer, Stephenie 11
mice 169, 170-1
microbes 5
midges 90
midnight horror tree 122-3
midsummer solstice 214-15
migration
  birds 84, 161-5, 237-8
  humans and circadian rhythms 240
  sea creatures 204, 206-7, 208
millipedes 109
monasteries 158
Monet, Claude *Charing Cross Bridge* 65
monuments and stone circles 214-19
the Moon
  atmosphere 5, 59
  lunar cycles 214
  lunar deities 213
  lunar eclipses 17
Moore, Thomas 122
morning twilight *see* dawn
mosquitoes 90
moths 7, 61, 121, 126, 127, 130, 171
  and bats 90-1, 98
  biofluorence 189
  hawkmoths 90-1, 98, 122, 127
  and light 233-4
  yucca moth 129
mouse-ear cress 134-5
Munch, Edvard 22-3
muscovy ducks 130
mythical beasts 8
mythologies of twilight 10, 220-3

INDEX

nautical twilight 29, 31, 32-3, 34, 35
   and the dawn chorus 145, 147-8
   lux levels 63
   swifts and twilight ascent 166-7
navigation
   magnetic deviation 86
   Viking sunstones 81-2, 85-6
newts 179, 236
nicotiana 100
nightingales 145, 157
noctule bat 89
nocturnal organisms 5, 61
North Pole 35-6
nyctinastic plants 100, 130-3

oceans
   bioluminescent creatures 196-203, 206
   and carbon emissions 208
   five layers or zones 195-6
   Forbes's 'Abyssus theory of marine life 204-5
   and light pollution 238
   marine snow 208
   mesopelagic layer 205, 206, 207
   navigation and Viking sunstones 81-6
   phytoplankton 204, 207-8
   sunlight zone 195, 204
   twilight zone 7, 193-208
   Valdivia Expedition and deep-sea exploration 205
   see also fish
octopus 196
Oedipus (Dryden and Lee) 77
the Otherworld 102-3
otters 6, 178-9
Ovid
   Metamorphoses 93-4

owlet moths 130
owls 104, 227, 235
   barn owls 6, 149-53, 169-71
   little owls 171-3
   tawny owls 170

Palaeolithic caves 219
peregrine falcons 165-6
Peru 216
petunias 124-5
pheasants 168
pheromones 76
phlox 115-16
photoreceptors 69, 71-5
phytoplankton 204, 207-8
pigbutt worm 197-8
pigs 41
Pinatubo, Mount 27
Pindar, Greek poet 103
pipistrelle bats 88, 89, 90, 97
plants 7, 119-35
   circadian rhythms 5, 61, 68, 69
   energy regulation 133-4
   fragrant 120-1, 124-6
   grasses 134
   light pollution 233, 234-5
   light-emitting plants 246
   nyctinastic 100, 130-3
   photoreceptors 70
   photosynthesis 133
   pollination 121, 126-30, 233
   stinking 122-4
   twilight pollination 121-2
   see also flowers
Platt, Phil 19-20
Pliny the Elder 158
polar darkness 35-6
polar twilights 71
polarised light 82-6
pollinators 121-2, 126-30
pollution 24

INDEX

ponds 6, 173, 174–90
  barn swallows 181
  daubenton's bat 182
  dragonflies 182–5
  frogs 174–6, 185, 186–7, 190
  insects 179–81
  tadpoles 184, 185, 190
  toads 174–5
poppies 128–9
poultry 136–42
  and artificial lighting 141–2
  see also chickens; cockerels
prayer plants 132
Purkinje, Jan Evangelista 115

quails 162–3
Quinault culture 220

rats 72
red flowers 115
reptiles 70, 121
robins 4, 144, 147–8
rodents 121, 171, 190
  and barn owls 149, 150, 152–3, 169, 170–1
Romans
  and cock crow 158, 159
Rossetti, Christina
  'When I am dead, my dearest' 247–8
Royal Society 86
  Krakatoa committee 23–4
Ruskin, John 24

Sackville-West, Vita 115–16
Scandinavian twilight 52–4
scents
  bats 99–100
  flowers 100
  fragrant plants 119–22, 124–6
schizophrenia patients 76

Scott, Walter
  'The Lady of the Lake' 103
Scripps Institute of Oceanography 194
sea angels 106
seabirds 204, 207
seals 201
Seasonal Affective Disorder 243
seasonal variations in twilight 33–6
Seven-stone Antas 216
Shakespeare, William
  Hamlet vii, 106, 159
  Macbeth 96, 110
  Measure for Measure 144
  A Midsummer Night's Dream 95, 102
  Romeo and Juliet 157–8
  Sonnet 73 226
shameplant 132
sharks 201
sheep 6–7, 134
shepherds 55
Shetland Islands 34–5, 42–3
ships 31
shrimp, fire-breathing 197
Siffre, Michel 65–8, 239
Simmer Dim 35
siphonophores 196
skies
  light and colour 24–6, 63–5
sleep and melatonin 241–2
slugs 107–9, 189
smell, human sense of 75–6
snails 107–9
social media 244
solstices 36, 215–16, 217–18, 219, 220
song thrushes 144
South American sac-winged bat 99–100
South Pole 35–6
Southern Circle 215

INDEX

sparrows 142-4, 147
'sparrow's fart' 159-60
spiders 189
spontaneous generation theory 177
spring 87-116, 136-53
squid 196, 202, 203, 207
   vampire squid 205
starlings 165-6
stars
   and ancient monuments 218
   and astronomical twilight 32
   and nautical twilight 31
   and navigation 31
stinkhorn fungus 123-4
stinking plants 122-4
Stoker, Bram
   Dracula 96
Stonehenge 214-15
stridulation 179, 180-1
Sturm, Christoph Christian 60
summer 35, 36
   changes in people's working lives 49
   midsummer solstice 36, 214-15, 219
   sunsets 26
the Sun
   and the Earth's atmosphere 17-18
   in Egyptian mythology 222
   and the ocean 196, 204
   and polarised light 84, 85
   rising and setting times 214
   solar deities 213
sundowning 244
sunlight, colours of 24-6, 63-5
sunrise 3-4, 10
   colours at 26
   cultural significance of 212, 220
   and the dawn chorus 147
   and photoreceptors 72
   seasonal variations in 33-5
   winter 38, 45
   see also dawn
sunset
   autumn 210-11
   colours at 26, 64-5
   cultural significance of 212-13, 220
   and photoreceptors 72
   and pond life 180
   seasonal variations in 33-5
   volcanic twilight 20-4
   winter 40, 45
   see also dusk
sunsets 4, 10
Sweden 53-4
Sweet, Robert 162, 165
Swift, Jonathan
   Directions to Servants 51, 52
swifts 166-7
swordfish 207

Tacitus
   Agricola 34
tadpoles 184, 185, 186, 190
tawny owls 170
Tennyson, Alfred Lord 22, 95
terminator line 59
terrapins 61
Thames, River 22
Theophrastus 69, 130
Thompson, Lawson 92
Thornborough Henges 217-19
thrips 121, 129
thrushes 4, 144, 147-8
tiger moths 130
toads 174-5, 187, 236
toadstools 61
touch, human sense of 76
tree sparrows 148
trees 167-8
   and artificial light 235

INDEX

tuna 201, 207
twilight years 225-6
Tyndall, John 24-5

vampire squid 205
vampires and bats 96
vegetables 129-30
Venus (planet) 211
vespertine organisms 61
Victorians and twilight 223-5
Viking sunstones 81-2, 85-6
Virgil 233
volcanic twilights 20-4, 26-7
voles 169, 170-1, 190

Wales
   Plygain religious service 158-9
wasps 129
watches 46
water boatmen 179, 180-1
Waterton, Charles 171-2
whales 69, 201, 202, 204
white plants 116
wild ducks 139
wildflowers 121

winter 35, 36, 38-56, 45-9
   midwinter solstice 36, 215-16, 217-18, 219, 220
   sunrise 38
   sunset 40
   temperatures 39
wisteria 120-1
witchcraft 110-11
wolves 55
women, folklore and bats 96-8
Wood, Neville 143
wood pigeons 144
wood witch 124
woodcocks 168
Woodhenge 215
woodland animals 6, 167-8
woodlice 90, 109
worms *see* earthworms
wrens 144

Yeats, W.B. 39
yucca plants 129

zeitgebers 62
Zoological Society 172

About the Author

SALLY COULTHARD is a bestselling author of over twenty-five books about natural history and rural life including *A Short History of the World According to Sheep*, *The Hedgehog Handbook* and *A Brief History of the Countryside in 100 Objects*. After studying Archaeology and Anthropology at Oxford, and working in factual television production, Sally moved back to her beloved Yorkshire, married a gardener and set up a smallholding; it's from there, surrounded by her family and other animals, that Sally writes from a shed in the old orchard.